Reinvent Your Business Model

Reinvent Your Business Model

How to Seize the White Space for Transformative Growth

Mark W. Johnson

Harvard Business Review Press

Boston, Massachusetts

The web addresses referenced in this book were live and correct at the time of the book's publication but may be subject to change.

Library of Congress Cataloging-in-Publication Data

Names: Johnson, Mark W., author.
Title: Reinvent your business model : how to seize the white space for
    transformative growth / by Mark W. Johnson.
Description: Boston, Massachusetts : Harvard Business Review Press, [2018] |
    Includes bibliographical references and index.
Identifiers: LCCN 2018002801 | ISBN 9781633696464 (hardcover : alk. paper)
Subjects: LCSH: Business planning—Case studies. | Strategic planning—Case
    studies. | Success in business—Case studies. | Organizational
    change—Case studies.
Classification: LCC HD30.28 .J655 2018 | DDC 658.4/012—dc23 LC record available at
    https://lccn.loc.gov/2018002801

For my mother, Adriana, who taught me

by example all the important things.

And for my beloved wife, Jane, and my children,

Kristina, Mark, Kathryn, Ella, and William.

They remind me every day what matters most.

The shift from oral to written speech is essentially a shift from sound to visual space . . . Because print controlled not only what words were put down to form a text but also the exact situation of the words on the page and their spatial relationship to one another, the space itself on a printed sheet—"white space" as it is called—took on high significance that leads directly into the modern and post-modern world.

—Walter Ong

CONTENTS

Part Three
Business Model Innovation as a Repeatable Process

Business Models and Innovation

More than a decade ago, Mark Johnson, SAP's Henning Kagermann, and I hashed out the principles of business model reinvention in the pages of the *Harvard Business Review*. A few years after that, Mark refined, clarified, and vastly expanded on our work in *Seizing the White Space*, a book that has proven itself to be even more relevant today, as new technologies continue to upend the marketplace. One of the most important and least understood insights that you'll derive from this book is that a new technology alone is not enough to propel a business into transformational growth. The business model that goes with it is absolutely key to its success or failure. I am delighted that the Harvard Business Review Press is reissuing it in this newly revised and updated edition, and proud to be able to introduce it. Mark was my student at Harvard Business School, and we went on to cofound the consultancy Innosight together. In the years since, he has become my teacher as well as my partner, which is about the most gratifying thing that any professor can say of a former student.

If our work on business model innovation has more than held up over the years, the term itself has become something of an empty cliché or buzz phrase, so much so that I have been tempted at times to retire it. That's a shame, because a deep understanding of the underlying principles of business models is an incredibly powerful tool, not just for management theorists but practitioners. Knowing how to build (or rebuild) a seamless business model is what allows the strongest leaders to stave off disruption from their competitors while driving innovation in their own enterprises.

Essentially, a business model can be broken down into four distinct elements:

1. A *value proposition*, which is to say, a product or service that does a job that customers need and that can be supplied to them at a price that they can afford.

2. *Resources*, which are the people, technology, facilities, equipment, funding, branding, and raw materials required to create the product or service and deliver it.

3. *Processes*, which are the means that people in organizations develop to produce and deliver products in repeatable, scalable, and sustainable ways.

4. A *profit formula*, which is how the company creates value for itself and its shareholders. It includes a revenue model (how much money can be made by selling how many products at a certain price), a cost structure (direct costs, overhead costs, and economies of scale), a target unit margin (how much must be netted from each transaction to achieve profitability), and resource velocity (how quickly resources need to be used to achieve profitability; for example, lead times, throughput, inventory turns).

I like to imagine that each of these four elements has a dial on it. When they are all set correctly, both the customer and the company receive what they need. However, between the time that the company designs, builds, and ships its first order and the time that it ships its 10 millionth, the settings on the dials will have been changed many times.

Those dials rarely change in isolation; if the setting on one conflicts with another, that other dial's setting must be changed as well. This is why "change," especially disruptive change, is so hard to do—because the more innovative a customer value proposition is, the less likely it is that it will be compatible with the resources, processes, and profit formulas that the business was originally built on. What this means in practice is that the new-and-different must be separated and even protected from the tried-and-true. As Mark says, "To play a new game on a new field requires a new game plan."

Mark takes the mystery out of business model innovation by laying out a structured, repeatable set of processes that lead in logical steps from brainstorming and initial planning to implementation, acceleration, and scaling—and he makes it all accessible by sharing case histories from real businesses. An admirably lucid thinker and a great explainer, with *Reinvent Your Business Model*, Mark Johnson has equipped a new generation of innovators with the insights and the tools that they need to seize the white spaces where the greatest opportunities lie.

—*Clayton M. Christensen*

Introduction

It has been eight years since this book was first published (under the slightly different title of *Seizing the White Space: Business Model Innovation for Growth and Renewal*). Much has happened in the business world since then. Blockbuster filed for bankruptcy in 2010 and closed all its remaining stores in 2013, a victim of Netflix's disruptive business model. A&P supermarkets (which the *Wall Street Journal* once dubbed "Walmart before Walmart") gave up the ghost in 2015, shortly after its 156th birthday. In June 2017, Whole Foods Market, which had done so much to upend the traditional business model for supermarkets, was acquired by Amazon, which has been turning the entire retail sector upside down over the past two decades.

Buffeted by competition from the iPhone and the tech giant Google's Android system, RIM's BlackBerry fell into a death spiral from which it never recovered. And in 2014, the Finnish tech giant Nokia sold its once world-beating mobile phone unit to Microsoft. Unable to stanch the unit's bleeding, Microsoft handed it off to Foxconn just two years later, writing off at least $9 billion. In 2015, Google reorganized itself under the umbrella of a new holding company it calls Alphabet (for *alpha bet*), redoubling its commitment to making big, winning wagers on what its cofounder Larry Page calls "the business of starting new things." Some of Google's new things (the aforementioned Android operating system, for example) have been alpha-plus; some (like Google Glass) have been duds. The gales of creative destruction never cease to blow.

What's been fascinating and gratifying to me over this near-decade, is seeing, again and again, how intensely important the art and science of business model innovation remains, and how relevant—indeed crucial—are the lessons that this book imparts. One point that I made in the first edition has been borne out repeatedly: digital transformation and business model innovation are not necessarily the same things.

Everyone is talking about digital transformation these days; in fact, it's become something of a catchphrase. But it's important to remember that simply adding a digital component to an existing business does not fundamentally transform it. New technologies can enable business model innovations, but the technology is just a means, not an end. As you will read in these pages, any number of well-designed, fully functional MP3 music players were available for purchase at the turn of the millennium, but they didn't make a dent in CD sales. It wasn't the advent of the iPod that transformed the music market; it was the new business model that Apple wrapped around it. Similarly, there were many electronic book readers on the market in the 1990s, but they were novelties. It wasn't until Amazon's Kindle debuted in 2007 with a business model that allowed readers to search Amazon's vast selection of titles and fill their devices with a single click that the ebook came into its own.

Giving a refrigerator the capability to take an inventory of its contents, or a wristwatch the capability to monitor its wearer's blood pressure, doesn't guarantee that consumers will line up to buy these products. New technology can no more ensure success than stamping "new and improved" on the packaging of a product can inoculate it against a competitor's new, cheaper, or better product that does a job that consumers really need. Absent a compelling customer value proposition, a powerful profit formula, and a set of key processes and resources that deliver the right product or service to the right people in the right way, even the most astounding new technologies can fail to gain traction in the marketplace. But with a fresh new business model, even a fully mature product can achieve dramatic new growth. Consider the humble taxicab. By making it possible for customers to summon and pay for rides with a smartphone app, a few tiny startups changed the face of the entire transportation industry. Since its launch in San Francisco in 2011, Uber now operates in sixty-six countries and 507 cities. Lyft was launched in the same city a year later and now operates in over 300 cities.

But the biggest lesson of all is that startups like Uber needn't have a monopoly on innovation. Big, established corporations can conceive, implement, test, and roll out world-changing products and services just as well as or even better than startups can. Not that it's easy. It takes real courage just to venture out into the uncharted white spaces where new opportunities lie. Even the sharpest-eyed business leaders have blind spots; the most visionary and even the most cautious are fallible and make mistakes. Though I believe that the tools and methods that I lay out in these pages will help your business home in on the most promising opportunities and incubate and exploit them with the highest degree of confidence, the process is never without risks.

As an author, I was naturally flattered when my publisher invited me to prepare an updated and revised second edition of this book. As a management thinker, I was even more excited to revisit the bold new ventures I wrote about ten years ago and see which had taken flight and which hadn't and why. For example,

Shai Agassi's Better Place initiative, a brilliantly envisioned and carefully thought-through system for electric cars, neither revolutionized the automobile industry nor made the world any greener; the company filed for bankruptcy in 2013. What went wrong? Looking through the lens of the Four-Box Business Model Framework, I will provide some answers. And of course, there are success stories too. The Liechtenstein-based toolmaker Hilti's ingenious business model, in which it transitioned from selling tools to contractors to leasing them, was flawlessly conceived and executed and allowed Hilti to achieve and sustain double-digit growth. Dow Corning's Xiameter—a low-touch, lower-cost way for customers to purchase large orders of silicon— has gone from strength to strength. I bring these and other case studies up-to-date in this new edition, delivering postmortems where appropriate. And in new chapter 6, I look at a number of successful digital transformations that have been undertaken since 2010. Of course, I have also made every effort to correct any errors that crept into the first edition.

Most importantly, I show you, step-by-step, how business model innovation can be done, systematically and repeatedly, from brainstorming to the blueprinting of a customer value proposition and profit formula, from incubating a new initiative to rolling it out and scaling it. If you take just one thing away from this book, I hope it's this: that business management at its best is so much more than executing already-existing business models—it is the art and science of exploring and discovering disruptive new ones that ensure a future of sustained growth and longevity.

I hope you enjoy the book and, most importantly, that you put its lessons to use.

Part One

A New Model for Growth and Renewal

1

The White Space and
Business Model Innovation

He who moves not forward, goes backward.

—Goethe

If you happened to be driving past a certain desolate airstrip in
Palmdale, California, one sunny morning in January 2006
and glanced out your window, you would have seen something
extraordinary—a large, lighter-than-air aircraft being readied for
flight.[1] This was not your usual blimp. It resembled three puffy hot
dogs strapped together and mounted on four round pillows—a
floating version, if you will, of the Oscar Mayer Wienermobile,
with large swinging fans protruding from each side and the rear.

Pulling your vehicle off the road, you would have watched in
amazement as this strange craft bounced and bumped down the
short runway, rose from the ground, and climbed to about four
hundred feet. Then, as its fans swung into action, you would have
seen it glide into a long gentle bank, turn back parallel to the

FIGURE 1

The Lockheed Martin P-791 hybrid airship

Photographs by Bob Driver and Gerhard Plomitzer.

runway, and cruise down its length, banking gracefully again at the other end and then flying in nose-first for a landing, leveling off before gently touching down on its four hovercraft-like pads.

Palmdale, a high desert community northeast of Los Angeles, is a typically sprawling exurb. Local residents know that the

Skunk Works, the famed R&D division of the aerospace giant Lockheed Martin, often uses this airstrip as a proving ground. The Lockheed Martin P-791, which was on its maiden flight that day, was a half-scale prototype of a hybrid airship that combines the aerostatic lift of its gas-filled body with the aerodynamic lift supplied by its winglike shape and forward propulsion to achieve flight.

As lumbering as it appears, this hybrid airship can do two very valuable things exceedingly well. First, it can take off and land in relatively small, unimproved spaces. Because it floats above the ground, it needs no runway in the conventional sense; it doesn't even require a smooth landing surface. Second, it can carry a very large payload, much larger than any helicopter or other short-takeoff-and-landing aircraft.[2]

As word of its successful flight spread, Lockheed Martin found itself fielding inquiries from a host of potential commercial customers for a product it had not yet decided to make. Management quickly realized that their experimental airship could generate substantial new growth for the company. Mining companies that want to extract valuable ore from remote locations, for instance, are often thwarted by the cost of transporting heavy extraction machinery to the sites. A hybrid airship could simply float the machinery in. In places like India, where poor road infrastructure inhibits reliable truck transport, packaged-goods manufacturers could use a hybrid airship to move large quantities of their products to previously inaccessible areas.

But despite its huge upside, the Lockheed Martin hybrid airship had yet to be commercialized when the first edition of this book was published in 2010, four years after potential purchasers had begun beating a path to its inventor's door. Why not? It should have been a slam dunk for Lockheed Martin, which is the same company that delivered the storied F-117 Nighthawk stealth fighter, the F-16 Fighting Falcon, and the F-35 Lightning II joint strike fighter. Did technical obstacles stand in the way, or were the financial hurdles too steep? Perhaps the problem was with Lockheed Martin itself.

VENTURING INTO THE WHITE SPACE

For decades, businesses of all stripes have wrestled with, failed to capitalize on, or passed over unique growth opportunities that don't seem to fit in with what they already do well. Just think of Xerox's Palo Alto Research Center (PARC), which famously owned the technologies that helped catapult Apple, Adobe, and 3Com to success. Why didn't Xerox exploit these technologies? More broadly, what underlying forces prevent great companies from embracing transformational opportunities?

Before we can answer that question, we must first understand something about where and how businesses tend to spend their time and resources in pursuit of new growth. At its most basic level, a company exists to deliver value in return for compensation. Every functioning company has a discrete sphere of operation—the activities it performs to serve customers and make a profit in return. Early in a company's life, this space may resemble an inkblot with no logical boundaries, flowing tentatively along the paths of least resistance. As a company matures, its operations become better defined and its borders more clearly established. Company efforts and capabilities become concentrated on this core operating space.

Over time, a successful company becomes very good at growing its core. It secures resources, improves existing products and creates new ones, expands markets, and increases efficiencies by improving processes, all to extract the most value from its core activities. It also continues to develop and refine the key business rules and metrics that ensure proper execution, establish discipline, and exert control throughout the organization. Either explicitly or implicitly, the company is operating according to a business model that defines the way it delivers value to its customers at a profit. Like a highly specialized organism, this model evolves until it perfectly suits the company's needs—showcasing its competitive strengths, honing its key resources and processes, and eliminating its vulnerabilities.

But what happens when an opportunity arises outside a company's core, an opportunity to serve a wholly new customer or an existing customer in a radically new way? What happens when an opportunity arises to create an entirely new market or to significantly transform an existing one? What of challenging new growth opportunities like the hybrid airship?

Many of these opportunities—even those that appear at first glance to be very different from the traditional core opportunity— fit quite well with the company's existing business model and are thus called *adjacencies*. But some require a company to fundamentally change its operations—adopting a different formula for making money, a new set of resources and processes, other expertise, and maybe a new way to coordinate and control activities. When such an opportunity arises—when delivering new value to the market requires you to reconsider the building blocks of your existing business model—that opportunity lies in your company's white space.

The term *white space* has been used before in business parlance to mean uncharted territory or an underserved market. But I use it to refer to the range of potential activities not defined or addressed by the company's current business model; that is, the opportunities that exist outside its core and beyond its adjacencies and that require a different business model to exploit. White space is a subjective valuation: one company's white space may be another company's core. What matters is that it describes activities that lie far outside a firm's usual way of working and presents a series of unique and perplexing challenges to that

FIGURE 2

Defining the white space

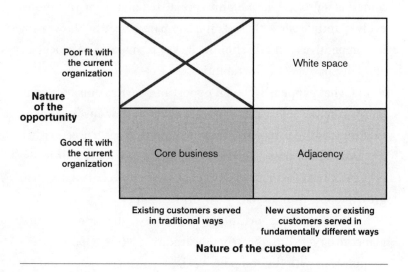

Nature of the customer

organization. It's an area where, relatively speaking, assumptions are high and knowledge is low—the opposite of conditions in the company's core space.

The chance to seize a piece of white space presents a tantalizing opportunity. Success can bring the transformational growth that business leaders seek. Yet understandably, a play for the white space feels risky, and often the numbers don't appear to add up. The market seems too foreign, or core capabilities don't apply. Some executives, having made one unsuccessful foray, just won't risk failing again.

LOCKHEED MARTIN'S WHITE SPACE

From Lockheed Martin's perspective, the commercial application of the hybrid airship lay far out in the white space. The firm's core operating space is the relatively low-volume, high-margin world of multibillion-dollar fighter aircraft, missiles, space satellites, and specialized integrated-systems work. From its beginning as a naval ship and airframe maker in the first half of the twentieth century, Lockheed (Lockheed Martin after it merged with Martin Marietta in 1995) has served government customers using government contracting systems. It excels at delivering extremely complex solutions in a highly structured way to a small number of clients. Everything it makes is built to order, and every step in the process—from systems development and safety testing to aircraft assembly—is tracked and billed against detailed requirements or specifications. This extreme structure means that margins are well defined in advance. Moreover, the defense industry's labyrinthine procurement process creates an effective barrier to entry for new rivals. As a result, Lockheed Martin occupies a relatively safe niche and has little incentive to stake out new territory. Sticking to its knitting has been a successful formula so far: everything Lockheed Martin does fits into four specialized business units—Aeronautics (military aircraft), Electronic Systems (military electronics and system integration), Information Systems & Global Services (US federal IT services), and Space Systems. Advanced Development Programs, as the Skunk Works is called today, is part of the Aeronautics unit.

The hybrid airship is in an entirely new, and far more mercurial, market space for Lockheed Martin. The company is accustomed to accurately projecting its products' potential markets, but since nothing like the hybrid airship has been built before, few existing metrics or market studies can predict its success. Making a significant investment in a product whose potential market size is merely assumed to be large seems irrational—especially since Lockheed Martin would probably have to shoulder the entire risk without government contract guarantees. Although comfortable with some types of uncertainty, the company has no processes for reducing the uncertainty of an unknown market.

Ironically, the very factors that signal the size of the opportunity are causes for concern in Lockheed Martin's world. To sell to the variety of customers that expressed interest in the P-791, the company would need to develop a wide range of new capabilities, including a commercial sales force and distribution channels, comfort and expertise operating in various cultures (mining, automotive, shipping, and the like), and a variety of marketing skills to reach multiple markets. Because commercial clients demand individual attention and each industry requires slightly different solutions, Lockheed Martin would also need to design a customizable offering, a far cry from its typically well-defined, fully specified military product. Finally, commercial ventures call for a completely different approach to managing finances, one that shares little with the government accounting standards, profit margins, and cash flow that drive the rest of Lockheed Martin's operations.

Those were the challenges—all legitimate and noteworthy—that confronted Lockheed Martin when the P-791 floated out of its hangar in Palmdale that sunny day in 2006. When the ship lumbered slowly down the runway and its Oscar Mayer body bore it gently into the sky, it lifted off into Lockheed Martin's white space, a very scary place to fly.

ACHIEVING SUSTAINED GROWTH

Former Lockheed Martin chair and CEO Norm Augustine once joked, "When it comes to diversification, the defense industry's record is unblemished by success."[3] While the hybrid airship clearly represents a thrilling opportunity for potentially transformational growth, that opportunity just as clearly lies many nautical miles from Lockheed Martin's core operating space. If you were Lockheed Martin, what would you do? Continue to target only your existing customers or take the risk of going where so many have failed before?

This is an untenable choice that no CEO should have to make. And as I now know, as I prepare the new edition of this book, Lockheed Martin did ultimately make that leap. In 2014, eight years after the P-791's successful test flight, Lockheed Martin entered into an agreement with Hybrid Enterprises of Atlanta, making it the exclusive reseller of its hybrid airships and the provider of aftermarket services—in other words, the provider of the sales, marketing, distribution, and customization capabilities that aerospace giant's core operations didn't have. Hybrid Enterprises began taking orders in 2015, with the first delivery scheduled for 2018.

In deciding never to go into the white space, you make up your mind that your company will walk away from all the opportunities the space contains—that you'll miss chances to transform an existing market, create a new one, or otherwise change the game in a powerful way to address competitors, disruptors, and industry discontinuities. Deciding never to venture into the white space leaves you with only your core and adjacencies to fuel your company's growth indefinitely.

If there ever was a time that a business could just execute year after year and achieve lasting success, that time is long past. Notwithstanding economic contractions or crises as large as the financial collapse of 2008, corporate stakeholders' expectations drive executives to plan for future growth, even as they batten down the hatches and try to ride out the storm. To be sure, businesses in their adolescent stages, when their products and systems are still relatively new, and more mature companies that have just made innovative leaps can rely on growth from the core for a long time. They can then move to adjacencies, creating new products and services to deliver on their financial targets, improving their tested formulas, better serving their existing customers, and even finding and serving new ones. When new market expansion slows down, process innovations can yield significant efficiencies and continued growth.

FIGURE 3

Defining the growth gap

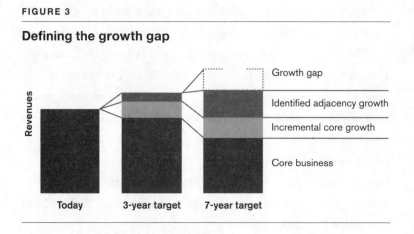

But there comes a time when established product lines fully mature, when process innovation reaches the upper thresholds of efficiency, and when new product development slows. Then companies face a looming shortfall—a growth gap—between their desired growth path and the growth that the existing business and envisioned adjacencies can deliver.[4] Commoditization, technological discontinuities, disruptive threats, changes in government policy or society's expectations, and intensified competition can all widen the growth gap, creating market conditions that significantly diminish the core's ability to grow.

Growth gaps are not new, but I would argue that they are becoming larger for more companies than ever before. Over the years, various business trends and management doctrines have emerged to address them. In the 1960s, many companies acquired undervalued but comparably sized companies in an attempt to buy growth. Although the rationale for conglomeration centered on the supposed benefits of scope of diversification, many acquisitions grew no faster—in fact, some grew slower—than before they were bought. Such attempts at growth amounted to little more than an accounting scheme, and when interest rates rose toward the end of the decade, most conglomerates were exposed for the bubble plays they were. With a few notable exceptions like General Electric, United Technologies, and Berkshire Hathaway, the majority of conglomerates lost value. By the mid-1970s, most had been broken up or greatly diminished.

In the late 1970s and early 1980s, companies seeking growth created tightly defined businesses that grew by expanding on their core expertise. Acquisitions were judged by how well they complemented the core. When growth from the core proved insufficient to meet the pressure for new growth, management thinking expanded again. Companies could grow through adjacencies.[5]

But as successful as the strategy of growth from the core and adjacencies has been in building solid, well-integrated businesses, it forgoes the white space, assuming defeat from the outset. This abundance of caution is a luxury that few companies can afford. Even more fundamentally than growth, most companies need renewal. They must evolve and deliver new sorts of value. That means leaving the comfort of their core and pursuing opportunities in their white space.

Seizing the white space requires new skills, new strengths, new ways to make money. It calls for the ability to innovate or reinvent the very theory of the business itself—a process that is known as *business model innovation*.

THE IPOD COMETH

One company that uncovered (perhaps inadvertently) the benefits of business model innovation was Apple. Once a major player in the personal computer market, Apple had watched its market share fall from 20 percent to less than 3 percent in the 1990s.[6] After the company struggled for years and finally settled into the role of a niche player, cofounder Steve Jobs returned from the business desert (where he'd been building a silly little animation company called Pixar) and vowed to put things right at Apple.

To refloat the sinking ship, Jobs followed the well-trodden path of product innovation, quickly rolling out the iMac (whose fashion-forward industrial design integrated its processor with the monitor) and the low-end iBook laptop. He also made sure that suppliers like Microsoft and Adobe continued to develop software for Apple. The new products were by all accounts smash hits, but they did little more than stanch the bleeding. You probably believe you know what happened next: in 2001, Apple introduced the iPod, the world's first digital music player, a product that revolutionized the way we consume entertainment, setting the company on the road to exponential growth. Jobs and his team pulled off a triumph of product development that changed the rules of the game.

Except that isn't what happened. Apple was not, in fact, the first company to bring a digital music player to market; that honor belongs to Diamond Media, which introduced the first MP3 player, the Rio, in 1998. Another company, Best Data, introduced its version of the MP3 player, the Cabo 64, in 2000.[7] So why did Apple's iPod revolutionize the music world? Was Apple's product better? Was its design more elegant? Well, those factors undoubtedly influenced consumers, but Diamond's and Best Data's products were also functional, portable, and stylish. In fact, the original iPod looked very much like the Rio's dial-controlled design.

Apple did something far smarter than wrap a good technology in a snazzy design; it wrapped a good technology in a great business model. Apple's genius lay in its realization that making it easy and convenient to download music would fuel demand for its high-priced music player. Eighteen months after introducing the iPod, Apple launched the iTunes Store, a service component that locked hardware, software, and digital music into one tightly woven, user-friendly package. This move recalled one of the great business model innovations of all time: King Gillette's revolutionary decision to give away the razor handle—a durable—to lock customers into purchasing his consumable, high-margin safety blades. Apple built on Gillette's model, essentially making the "blades" (high-volume iTunes music with good margins) more accessible than ever before while also locking in the purchase of the "razor handle" (the iPod itself), with high margins returning high profits.[8]

This business model, substantially different from anything Apple had done before, defined value in a new way. The success of this business model innovation rejuvenated—indeed transformed—Apple. In just three years, the iPod/iTunes combination became a $10 billion product, accounting for nearly half the company's revenue. Apple's market capitalization skyrocketed from around $5.4 billion at the end of its fiscal year 2002 to $133 billion at the end of 2007, during the key years of the iPod/iTunes combination's growth.[9] What's more, the company's digital platform became the basis of a newly defined Apple brand. No longer was Apple simply one competitor among many in the rapidly commoditizing PC hardware space. It became a leader in the then brave new world of lifestyle media. Its new business model paved the way for further evolution, as Apple subsequently moved into video content and convergent media.

It would be easy to think that the iPod and iTunes combination was a natural fit for Apple, that it was a low-risk extension of the company's core expertise in hardware and software systems integration. But the transformation actually represented business model reinvention, a real white-space move. Apple had been a computer maker. It had limited experience with the world of music and media and virtually no identity in the public's mind as a provider of entertainment technology. Sony's Walkman line had dominated the portable-music market since the early 1980s.[10] In fact, the music industry was deeply suspicious of MP3 technology, which it rightly feared would cannibalize the CD market. To enter hostile territory and propose an unproven technology

FIGURE 4

The impact of iPod/iTunes on Apple's growth

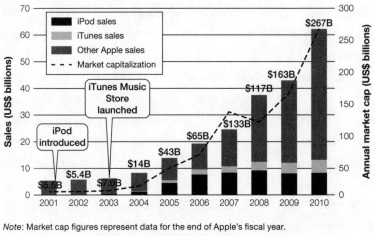

Note: Market cap figures represent data for the end of Apple's fiscal year.

Source: Apple 10k 2003-2010; ycharts.com; Innosight analysis.

with little or no track record in the space was risky indeed. Such a move would have been impossible if Apple hadn't devoted as much creative energy to innovating its business model as it did to its products.

SEIZING THE WHITE SPACE WITH BUSINESS MODEL INNOVATION

Business model innovations have reshaped entire industries, redistributing billions of dollars of value. In retail, discounters that, like Target, Walmart, and Amazon, entered the market with innovative business models accounted for 93 percent of the total industry market capitalization by 2016, having seized more than $300 billion of value from their old-line competitors.[11] More than half of the thirty-nine companies founded since 1984 and on the *Fortune* 500 between 2006 and 2016 made this list through business model innovation.[12]

FIGURE 5

Business model innovation in US retailing

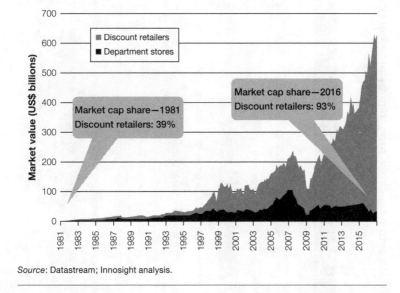

Source: Datastream; Innosight analysis.

It's no wonder, then, that business model innovation has become such an executive buzz phrase. A 2014 Boston Consulting Group survey polled fifteen hundred senior executives. More than fourteen hundred stated that their companies had attempted some degree of business model innovation.[13] Yet for all the buzz, and despite the talent and resources at their disposal, companies that attempt it rarely succeed. No more than 10 percent of innovation investments at global companies are currently focused on developing new business models; most successful innovative business models are forged by startups.[14]

With all its immense promise and high-level attention, why do so few big companies manage to translate business model innovation into action? They can't pull it off because, as familiar as the term is, very few people really understand what a business model is (and what it isn't). Nor do they understand which model

FIGURE 6

Companies founded since 1984 that entered the *Fortune* 500 with a business model innovation between 2006 and 2016

Company	Description
Alaska Air Group	Airline with focus on regional operations in the Pacific Northwest
Broadcom Corporation	"Fabless" semiconductor maker (one that outsources its manufacturing to Asian subcontractors)
Cognizant Technology Solutions Corporation	Provider of global IT consulting and business process outsourcing services
Community Health Systems	Hospital operator that provides health-care services primarily in underserved, nonurban markets
DaVita HealthCare Partners	Provides dialysis services for patients suffering from chronic kidney failure. Specialists operate in outpatient centers
Discover Financial Services	Operates on a closed-loop lending model, in which it extends credit to Discover card holders, collects interest on the aggregate loan balance, and collects processing fees
Dollar Tree	Discount retailer that sells liquidated and generic products to price-conscious shoppers
Expedia	Online travel service that connects travelers with excess hotel capacity, particularly in the US domestic market
GameStop Corp.	Developer of a retail model for video games that is now expanding into cellphones, computers, and collectibles
Genesis Healthcare	Operator of nursing centers and assisted/senior living residences, and provider of short-term post-acute rehabiliation therapies
JetBlue Airways Corporation	Low-cost airline carrier that positioned itself as a value player by using New York City's JFK airport as its hub, purchasing a new fleet of Airbus A-320s, and providing snacks and video entertainment rather than full meals

Company	Description
Las Vegas Sands Corporation	Real estate developer that was the first to combine hotels with conference centers, maximizing midweek occupancy rates
LifePoint Health	Provider of health-care services in growing regions, rural communities, and small towns
Murphy USA	Operator of 1,100 low-cost retail gas stations built next to Walmart locations
NetApp	Provider of software-enabled data management and storage solutions
Netflix	Pioneer video rental subscription service that operated first by mail, then by online streaming; now venturing into video production
PayPal Holdings	One of the first digital payment intermediaries, allowing users to make purchases through a click or an email
Priceline Group	Online travel service that helps hotels fill excess capacity with a "Name Your Price" model that reduces friction for consumers and allows Priceline to collect the spread
Quanta Services	A national network that provides engineering and construction services to electric utility and telecom companies
Salesforce.com	First major software-as-a-service provider; allows businesses to access cloud-based software on a subscription basis
SanDisk Corporation	Pioneer in NAND data storage technologies that provides flash memory to retail consumers and OEMs
Steel Dynamics	Mini-mill operator that produces steel from scrap metal instead of iron ore
United Rentals	National tool rental service that provides construction and industrial equipment to companies, utilities, municipalities, and homeowners

their organization is operating under or how they would go about creating a new model and why or when they should.

The solution to this perplexing challenge is revealed in the pages ahead. In chapter 2, I will define the elements of a successful business model and explain how they interrelate. Part 2 addresses the market circumstances that open up opportunities and imperatives to seize the white space through business model innovation. In this part of the book, I will explore how business model innovation can empower organizations to transform existing markets, create new ones, or recast whole industries—and how new business models can deploy cutting-edge, enabling technologies for transformative growth. Finally, in part 3, I lay out in detail a structured process for designing new business models and developing them into profitable, thriving enterprises. I also investigate the managerial and behavioral challenges that commonly thwart unguided forays into the unknown.

This book shows you how you can turn business model innovation into a managed process and a more predictable discipline. When we're done, I hope that you will thoroughly understand how great business propositions are constructed and recognize that even the most traditional company can achieve transformational growth and renewal.

To play a new game on a new field requires a new game plan. Business model innovation will give you a language and framework for understanding both the core space of your existing enterprise and the white space you hope to seize. Think of this as your playbook for conquering the unknown.

The Four-Box Business Model Framework

The structure of language determines not only thought but reality itself.

—Noam Chomsky

In his seminal book *An Actor Prepares*, the great drama coach Konstantin Stanislavsky tells the story of an actor who is asked to hide under a table when, according to a stage direction, an imminent threat is just offstage. An actor's job, of course, is to draw on his life experience to create real emotions and actions within the imagined confines of a script and a stage. This actor was trying to find the emotional motivation to dive under the table, but he could not convince himself that he was truly afraid. Unable to feel the fear, he couldn't perform.

"Do not think," the master teacher told him. "Just dive under the table and cover your head."

The actor did so.

"What do you feel?" the teacher asked.

"I feel afraid," said the student.

"Sometimes you feel afraid and you dive under the table," the master concluded, "but sometimes, if you dive under the table, you will feel afraid."[1]

Stanislavsky's great contribution to Western art was to propose that while creative inspiration often leads to structure, structure just as often unlocks creativity.

The same dynamic holds true for business model innovation. The main reason most companies fail at creating new businesses is that they fear to act without an unambiguous motive to do so. Staffed with people trained to operate within the defined norms of their company and their industry, these firms shy away from moves that don't immediately make sense within the context of their current operations. Like the actor who could not dive under the table unless it made emotional sense for him to do so, they resist venturing into the unknown territory of business model innovation when so much uncertainty clouds the path to success. Who knows what's under the table? And who is willing to risk his job to find out?

Occasionally, a visionary leader—a Jeff Bezos or a Steve Jobs—intuitively understands what it takes to innovate a business model or to build an entirely new one. The rest of us need an explicit framework and a manageable process to reduce the uncertainty and risk of venturing into the unknown. As Stanislavsky taught, we need structure to unlock our creativity—a disciplined process that can spur us toward new ideas. The better we understand the structure of business models, the better we will be at creating them.

A business model, in essence, is a representation of how a business creates and delivers value for a customer while also capturing value for itself, doing so in a repeatable way. Of course, the notion of how value is created and delivered is fundamental; but strangely, businesses can rarely articulate it clearly. Most leaders don't sufficiently understand their company's existing business model, the premise behind its development, its natural interdependencies, or its strengths and weaknesses when in pursuit of new growth. They simply don't know if they should use their core business and established model to deliver on a new customer opportunity or if that proposition is a move into a white space that requires a new model. Value remains curiously implicit, as if it were some guiding presence that hovers somewhere above the surface of the enterprise. Indeed, the consequent clumsiness in creating new business models has led to the widespread belief that companies can only successfully innovate close to the core.

Part of the problem is a lack of a shared vocabulary. Thought leaders in the past have offered numerous definitions of a business model. The late management guru Peter Drucker implicitly defined it as "the theory of the business."[2] Management consultant and author Joan Magretta described business models as "stories that explain how enterprises work."[3] Other management theorists and practitioners have devised frameworks, some of which focus purely on the economics of a business, while others take an impossibly wide scope, including almost every aspect of business strategy and organization.[4] Few, if any, squarely focus on the elements in the business system that are central to the creation and delivery of value and the way those elements work together to ensure or impede the overall success of the enterprise.

To render the most essential elements of value creation in clear language, I propose a four-box framework. I believe it provides the structure needed to reveal and categorize all the issues that must be addressed before a company can confidently venture into the low-knowledge, high-assumption environment of its white space. Employed methodically, the framework will give you a road map to new possibilities for innovation, transformational growth, and renewal that you never thought you could capitalize on before.

FIGURE 7

The four-box business model

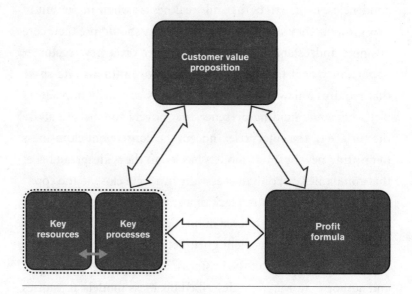

THE FOUR KEY ELEMENTS OF A BUSINESS MODEL

The basic architecture underlying all successful businesses consists of four interdependent elements that can be represented with four boxes. Every thriving enterprise is propelled by a strong *customer value proposition* (CVP)—a product, service, or combination thereof that helps customers more effectively, conveniently, or affordably do a job that they've been trying to do. The CVP describes how a company creates value for a given set of customers at a given price. The *profit formula* defines how the company will capture value for itself and its shareholders in the form of profit. It does this by distilling an often-complex set of financial calculations into the four variables most critical to profit generation: revenue model, cost structure, target unit margin, and resource velocity. Finally, *key resources* and *key processes,* are the means by which the company delivers the value to the customer and to itself. These critical assets, skills, activities, routines, and ways of working enable the enterprise to fulfill the CVP and profit formula in a repeatable, scalable fashion.[5] When properly integrated with and fully congruent with the CVP and profit formula, they provide the essence of a company's competitive advantage. Every successful company is fulfilling a real customer job-to-be-done with an effective, well-integrated business model, whether it knows it or not.[6]

The power of this deceptively simple framework lies in the complex interdependencies of its parts. Successful businesses devise a relatively stable system in which these elements interact in consistent and complementary ways. A change to any one of the four affects all the others and the system as a whole. Incongruities or conflicts between elements, even seemingly inconsequential ones, can bring about its downfall. There are also guiding rules and metrics that govern the business model and its associated major elements, which we will discuss in more detail in the last chapter.

But first, let's examine each element (or box) more closely.

CUSTOMER VALUE PROPOSITION (CVP)

A customer value proposition helps customers more effectively, reliably, conveniently, or affordably solve an important problem (or satisfy a job-to-be-done) at a given price.

A powerful, focused CVP is the keystone of all successful business models. A great CVP identifies an important, unsatisfied consumer problem, or "job," and then proposes a focused product or service (or combination) that delivers it in the right way at a given price. Before you can design a great CVP, you must first thoroughly understand your target customer's job-to-be-done.

As Harvard Business School professor Theodore Levitt first pointed out, customers do not really buy products—they hire

FIGURE 8

Customer value proposition (CVP)

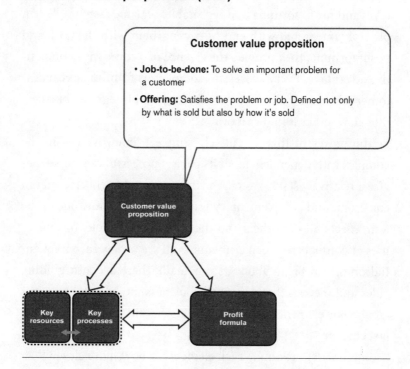

them to accomplish particular tasks.[7] He famously said that people don't go to the hardware store to buy a drill, for instance; they go there to buy a hole. The drill they purchase is the candidate they hire to get that job done.[8] Over the last few decades, a lot of emphasis has been put on "customer needs" and "the voice of the customer." But understanding a customer's job-to-be-done is not the same as understanding a customer. Too often, "needs" are defined too broadly or, worse, are thought of only in relation to existing products and services. To develop new CVPs in the white space, you must stop trying to figure out what kinds of products people are trying to buy and instead work out what they are trying to get done in a given circumstance.

To illustrate, let's consider the cell phone and its cousin, the smartphone. A cell phone addresses the job "I want to conveniently make phone calls when I'm on the go, away from my home or office."[9] If you ask people why they chose a smartphone rather than a cell phone, most will say something like, "I don't just want to communicate; I also want to organize my life on the go." Because no other gadget performed these functions and satisfied this job-to-be-done, the first smartphones became very popular. Palm, Research in Motion (RIM, the maker of the BlackBerry), and other vendors built their businesses by providing better calendars, faster connections, and easier email applications to address this job.

Now think about the last time you attended an overly long business meeting, had spare time in an airport between connections, or waited for your lunch at a restaurant. In those moments, your job-to-be-done was different: "Help me kill small snippets of time in useful ways." That job could be fulfilled by many means. You could read a magazine or newspaper, watch TV in the airport bar, listen to a recorded book, or scribble a memo. A smarter smartphone could provide even more useful and more convenient alternatives—easily accessible stock quotes, say, or news headlines, games that you could play quickly, chat functions, Twitter access, and the like. This new job-to-be-done called for a new CVP, and the Apple iPhone—with a full web browser and a host of downloadable applications to suit every taste—offered it, in the process redefining just how smart a smartphone could be.

Learning from its past success with the iPod, Apple again embraced a sales-and-service model and built the App Store, which hosts products from a diverse community of third-party developers. Competing for this second job-to-be-done changed the market for smartphones, and following Apple's success, RIM, Palm, and other competitors rushed to follow suit. Unfortunately for them, they never came close to catching up with Apple. Palm teetered close to bankruptcy before it was sold to HP in 2010; RIM, now known as BlackBerry, hoped its BlackBerry 10 would spark its comeback in 2013, but the device fell far short of expectations.

Identifying an important job-to-be-done requires adopting a proactive, outside-in approach (which I will discuss in more detail in chapter 7), for, as Drucker famously noted, "The customer rarely buys what the company thinks it is selling him."[10] With effort, every job-to-be-done can be precisely defined and categorized.

Once you fully understand the various dimensions of the job-to-be-done, you can design an offering that fulfills that job in a unique way. An offering is a product, service, or some combination made available at an affordable price. Included in the concept of an offering is the experience of purchasing, using, and maintaining it. Sometimes, for instance, a job can be satisfied more by how something is sold than by what is sold. The first plain-paper photocopier, the iconic Xerox 914, languished when it was introduced in the 1960s. Companies didn't want to pay a high price for an unproven technology. So Xerox president Joe Wilson borrowed an idea from IBM and offered to lease the machines instead, charging a per-copy usage fee.[11] Business skyrocketed.

The job-to-be-done and the offering (product or service, means of access or distribution, price) combine to form the CVP for any successful business model. Its overall value derives from three key metrics:

1. How important the job-to-be-done is to customers

2. How satisfied customers are with current solutions

3. How well the new offering gets the job done, relative to the other options

The more important the job, the better the match between the job and the offering, the generally lower the offering's price,

FIGURE 9

The customer value proposition formula

How do you maximize a CVP?	1 Identify an important job-to-be-done that is poorly satisfied today for a customer	then	2 Devise and develop an offering that does the job better than alternatives at the lowest appropriate price

and the greater the overall value generated for the customer from the CVP.[12]

Identifying important unfulfilled jobs—the first critical step in developing a new CVP—often requires close observation. Imagine, for a moment, that it is 2008 and that you are Keyne Monson, a medical devices executive and social entrepreneur. You are standing on a hot, dusty sidewalk in Calcutta, watching the people go by. Whether they know it or not, a disturbingly high percentage of them are suffering from cardiac diseases (India, which makes up 16 percent of the world's population, accounts for more than half the globe's heart disease—in fact, an Indian dies of heart failure almost every thirty seconds).[13] You know of a product, the implantable cardiac pacemaker, that could improve and indeed save many of these lives. Medtronic, which manufactures it, has tasked you to devise a business model that would allow it to enlarge its footprint in India. But relatively few Indians have access to advanced medical care, have the medical insurance to pay for it, or, for that matter, even know that such things as pacemakers exist. Clearly, there is a need to provide greater awareness, access, and affordability for Medtronic's pacemaker product and the associated diagnostic and surgical services, allowing more Indians to benefit from them.

At the other end of the market and the other side of the world, John Mackey, cofounder and CEO of the natural-foods retailer Whole Foods Market, looked out on a different sort of street. This one is traveled by relatively well-off food aficionados, middle-aged baby boomers who have grown increasingly conscious of their health, shoppers interested in sustainable consumption, and health-food consumers. Like Monson, Mackey discerned in this traffic jam of disparate general-merchandise customers an unserved job-to-be-done. These otherwise unconnected consumer groups all wanted a very high grade of fresh perishables—organic produce, cruelty-free meat, wild-caught fish, and the like—not widely available in local supermarkets. They wanted to live healthier lives and consume tastier and more sustainable food, but most lacked access to the scattered farmers' markets and specialty stores that could make these desires possible. Available solutions were not good enough to serve their job-to-be-done.

At the time, Whole Foods was one of those small providers, a regional chain of health-food stores that catered to the naturopathic-conscious consumer niche. Mackey believed that if the stores could furnish a superior grade of perishables, then the much larger group of food connoisseurs and green buyers would also find Whole Foods' core natural and naturopathic products appealing. Making the supermarket consumption experience more pleasurable would further add to the appeal.

So Whole Foods reached out from its crunchy-granola core to serve a customer looking for a new focused job-to-be-done: "Give me full and pleasurable access to a variety of foods and products that meet my high standards for quality and honor my interests in health, organics, and protecting the environment."[14] The company built a CVP to address a job-to-be-done for which high-end consumers were willing to pay a premium.

Simplicity and elegance drive the formulation of great CVPs. Their power lies in their clarity, but clarity can be difficult to achieve. All too often, rather than focusing on a single job, companies attempt to fulfill many jobs at once. In doing lots of things, they do nothing very well.

Focused CVPs are as important for what they rule out as for what they rule in. By concentrating on jobs-to-be-done, a well-defined CVP helps overenthusiastic innovators resist the temptation to overload offerings with features that customers don't want to buy (and will resent paying for).

If you can't describe your CVP in a few sentences that non-businesspeople can understand, then it is not clear or focused enough. Focused CVPs yield focused new business models, and a well-defined new business model allows incumbents to better understand when they need to replace their existing model to reach new target customers.

PROFIT FORMULA

A profit formula is the economic blueprint that defines how the company will create value for itself and its shareholders. It specifies the assets and fixed cost structure, as well as the margins, volume, and velocity that are required to cover them.

It's not simply finding a new way to make money that can revolutionize an industry; a powerful CVP allows companies to generate profits in revolutionary ways. The profit formula defines the gross and net margins the organization must achieve, given the structure and magnitude of the fixed and variable costs inherent in its resources. The formula specifies how big the organization must become to break even and the pattern of profit improvement, if any, that comes with increasing scale. With its profit formula, an organization defines how fast it must turn over its assets to achieve adequate returns. In retailing, for example, companies like R. H. Macy and Federated Department Stores found success with a high-touch CVP whose profit formula involved high markups and low inventory turns.

FIGURE 10

Profit formula

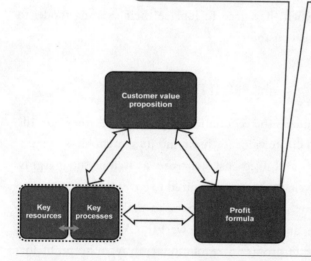

> • **Revenue model:** How much money can be made: price × quantity. Quantity can be thought of in terms of market share, purchase frequency, ancillary sales, etc.
> • **Cost structure:** Includes direct costs, overhead costs, and economies of scale
> • **Target unit margin:** How much each transaction should net to cover overhead and achieve desired profit levels
> • **Resource velocity:** How quickly resources need to be used to support target volume. Includes lead times, throughput, inventory turns, asset utilization, etc.

Customer value proposition

Key resources   Key processes

Profit formula

When catalog companies like Sears came along, profit formulas entailed a lower markup, but the companies could turn inventory much faster to make similar aggregate profits. Then a major revolution started in the 1950s with the emergence of discount retailers like E. J. Korvette and Zayre in the northeast United States, then Aldi in Germany, and eventually Kmart and Target throughout the United States. To offer lower prices than department stores and mail-order houses, discount retailers needed to lower the markup on their merchandise even further. To do that and still make a profit, they needed to generate higher inventory

FIGURE 11

Shifting profit formulas in the retail industry

	Department stores	Catalog retailers	Discount retailers	Online-only retailers
Average markup over cost of inventory	40%	30%	23%	5%
Inventory turns	3x	4x	5x	25x
Return of inventory invested (markup × inventory turns)	120%	120%	115%	125%

Source: Clayton Christensen and Richard Tedlow, "Patterns of Disruption in Retailing," Harvard Business Review, January–February 2008.

turns—in other words, move more product more quickly through their stores.

The discount retailers initially achieved a lower overall cost structure by focusing on hard goods that sell themselves. This focus allowed the discount stores to substantially reduce one of the highest costs in retailing—service personnel.[15] Then discount retailing went even further when it jumped online. Companies like Amazon could generate profits with even less of a markup by turning inventory even faster.

Since Amazon dramatically improved how fast inventory moved through its system, it also maximized the return from its working capital. And it shifted the cash flow from a seller-financed model to a buyer-financed one.[16] Before Amazon, book retailers paid publishers for merchandise 90 days after they received it but on average held it in inventory for 168 days, essentially carrying the cost of the product for 78 days. Combining internet technology with just-in-time supply-chain management, Amazon changed that fundamental dynamic. Instead of 168 days, Amazon held a book in inventory an average of just 17 days.[17] Even though Amazon agreed to pay publishers sooner than the industry standard—in about 58 days—its profit formula created a float that kept the customer's

FIGURE 12

Amazon versus traditional book retailer

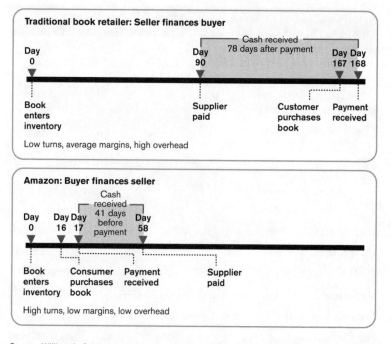

Source: William A. Sahlman and Laurence E. Katz, "Amazon.com—Going Public," Case 9-899-033 (Boston: Harvard Business School Publishing, 1998), 22.

money in its hands for an average of 41 days. Doing so enabled Amazon to survive while e-tailing was still a relatively low-volume channel and then to thrive as the sector achieved scale.

Four key variables determine the success of a profit formula. These variables are tightly interrelated and work together to clearly define the ways that value can be created for the company and its shareholders, and are therefore critical to predicting the success of a new business model.

Revenue Model

The revenue model is the offering price multiplied by the quantity sold. The profit formula is tightly linked to, and significantly defined by, the CVP because the offering price is an essential part of both. In the CVP, the offering price is a key quantifier of value. Its role in the profit formula depends on whether the company is devising a low-end or a premium business.

In low-cost business models, price is a key starting point for determining the profit formula. Medtronic had to make its product affordable even to poorer, uninsured Indians. To do that, it needed to get to a price point significantly below the $30,000-plus that pacemakers are sold for in the United States and other developed countries. Medtronic also needed to provide consumers with inexpensive, easy-to-obtain financing.

In premium businesses, the price tends to be dictated by the cost of the resources needed to deliver the CVP. Whole Foods, for instance, knew that it needed to offer a superior grade of perishables to deliver on its CVP, which led it to devise a profit formula that involved higher-end pricing.

Quantity (or volume)—can be measured in various ways, such as market share or projected sales. Service businesses typically measure it as the time taken to perform a service or the number of transactions; manufacturers generally use quantity sold. A comprehensive approach to defining quantity asks three questions:

1. How many customers will I have?

2. How many units per customer per transaction will I sell?

3. How many transactions per customer can I expect?

The first question goes to the potential of the customer addressed by the CVP. The other two define the type of offering developed to satisfy the job-to-be-done.

A further question you should consider in this connection is how much additional income you can project from related products or services. It isn't strictly a part of the cost structure of the offering, but income from related offerings has an important bearing on the business model's long-term success. In 2010, for example, Apple controlled nearly 70 percent of the MP3 player market but anticipated declining sales as the market reached its saturation point.[18] But by raising its song prices, it kept its ancillary income from music sales in sharp ascent. This was significant, as Apple had become the largest music retailer in the world.[19]

Cost Structure

The cost structure is simply made up of direct costs and overhead, taking into account economies of scale. Successful companies typically have well-defined cost structures; overhead requirements in particular are very difficult to change. So business leaders have a strong impulse to start with existing overhead costs when devising the cost structure of a new business model. But the overhead-first order is backward. In the new business model, the overhead must be determined by the requirements of the value proposition, not taken as a given.

Target Unit Margin

The target unit margin is the operating profit per unit required to cover overhead costs and achieve the desired profit level at the target volume. Strictly speaking, it's an outgrowth of the revenue model and the cost structure, but I call it out here separately because it's used so often in many companies as a proxy for the entire profit formula. Looking at margins in isolation and worrying that a new business model's margins will be too low, incumbents can miss out on transformational growth opportunities. Smaller margins set off alarm bells for many companies' strategists and finance people; they are quick to block initiatives that don't meet the margins of the core business model, fearing that they will fail to meet overhead. But margins are only a part of an overall profit formula—the goal is not necessarily to maintain any certain margin but to achieve the margin needed to reap the target profits.

Resource Velocity

Resource velocity defines how quickly resources need to be used to support target volume. It specifies not just the number of widgets a business can make, but how many it can invent, design, produce, warehouse, ship, service, sell, and pay for throughout the value chain for a given amount of investment during a given period. Similar to asset turnover, this variable includes not only the actual turnover of current assets like inventory but also the ability of the overhead or other related resources and established processes to support the planned turnover. Resource velocity is an extremely important factor that, as Amazon's example demonstrates, is often overlooked.

Resource velocity is the answer to the question "How will we achieve volume production?" It determines the overall capacity of the entire business model to serve the CVP. The greater the resource velocity of a business, the more of its offering the business can produce. Innovations that increase resource velocity allow you to make acceptable aggregate profits at lower gross-unit margins.

Like overhead in the cost structure, resource velocity tends to be very rigid in existing business models. Everything, from floor space and the physical proximity of parts to the production line to overhead operations, has been carefully planned out and tends to be taken as immutable. For this reason, incumbents unnecessarily (and sometimes fatally) limit their horizons when considering the feasibility of new opportunities, since those designs may not work for a new CVP. Too often, companies reject the new CVP when that happens, rather than explore the possibility of constructing a comprehensive new business model that would make the proposition profitable.

Each element in a profit formula profoundly influences the others. For example, Medtronic knew that drastically reducing the price of its pacemakers required accepting a sharp reduction in gross-unit margins and engineering a concurrent reduction in the full-cost structure. However, Medtronic was developing a long-term business model and associated profit formula that would significantly increase sales volume and the supporting resource velocity. Further, high profits were not Medtronic's ultimate concern; its goals were scale and sustainability—the business model it created in India is a template that will allow it to provide its lifesaving technology in other emerging economies and for poorer, underserved patients in developed nations. Medtronic's mission, as CEO Omar Ishrak puts it, is to "extend life, alleviate pain, and restore health using our technologies. And this applies to all people around the world. Going into emerging markets is not only an important opportunity, it's a responsibility."[20]

The key to profitability for Whole Foods lay in shifting more of its sales volume to areas of the store that produced higher margins. The traditional revenue-generating, high-volume areas of supermarkets are the center aisles. Most markets offer perishables—vegetables, milk, meat, and cheese—at low margins to attract customers, banking that they will also buy large amounts of the more profitable dry goods and supplies. Whole Foods' target customers, by contrast, are willing to pay higher prices for high-quality, often organic, fresh perishables and prepared foods, shifting volume and much of the profitability to the periphery of the store.[21] Although they also want the natural and organic dry goods, these customers purchase far fewer of these items than they would in a nonspecialty supermarket.

Mainstream supermarkets keep costs low through a system of highly organized, central distribution networks. Natural-food suppliers, in contrast, tend to be small, local producers. Whole Foods' higher direct food costs, greater management complexity, and need to coordinate numerous low-volume suppliers add up to high overhead costs. Selling more perishables and prepared foods and fewer commodity items means lower overall inventory turns, furthering the need for greater markup overall.

Essentially, Whole Foods inverted the established supermarket model. It relies not on volume but on higher prices and higher margins on the perishables, which its customers buy in large quantities.[22] To sell customers on higher prices, it invests heavily in making the grocery-shopping experience more pleasurable and less tiresome. By considering the customer experience an integral part of its CVP and devising the appropriate profit formula to satisfy it, Whole Foods commands the higher margins it needs to satisfy its customers' job-to-be-done. People often believe a company's profit formula is its business model. This is understandable, since at the end of the day (or more precisely, the end of the fiscal year), every company hopes to have generated profit. But truly, the profit formula is only one element of the total business model.

KEY RESOURCES AND KEY PROCESSES

Key resources are the unique people, technology, products, facilities, equipment, funding, and brand required to deliver the value proposition to the customer. Key processes are the means by which a company delivers on the CVP in a sustainable, repeatable, scalable, and manageable way.

Although the delivery of a CVP usually requires a vast array of resources, just a few key resources spell the difference between success and failure. You need to ask, "What unique combination of personnel, technology, products, facilities, equipment, suppliers, distribution channels, funding, and brand are needed to

FIGURE 13

Key resources and processes

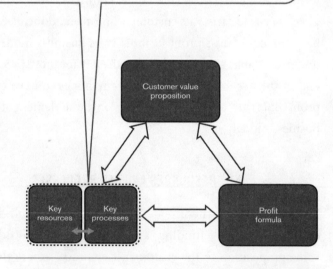

Key resources needed to deliver the CVP profitably. Might include:

- People
- Technology, products
- Equipment
- Information
- Channels
- Partnerships, alliances
- Funding
- Brand

Key processes, as well as business rules, behavioral norms, and success metrics that make the profitable delivery of the CVP repeatable and scalable. Might include:

- **Processes**: Design, product development, sourcing, manufacturing, marketing, hiring and training, IT
- **Business rules and success metrics**: Margin requirements for investment, credit terms, lead times, supplier terms
- **Behavioral norms**: Opportunity size needed for investment, approach to customers and channels

Customer value proposition

Key resources

Key processes

Profit formula

support the CVP within the constraints of the envisioned profit formula?" People are the critical resource to a professional services firm. A consumer packaged-goods company might focus on its brand and channel retailers. As the world becomes more connected, companies no longer have to house all their own key resources; more and more look to partners to provide what they need. Consider, for example, Apple's industry-shifting partnership with Foxconn. The contract manufacturer handles production and assembly of the iPhone and other Mac products, often investing in state-of-the-art manufacturing techniques to meet Apple's specific aesthetic standards. The partnership frees Apple to focus on its core design and marketing expertise.[23]

Key processes are the recurrent, critical tasks—such as manufacturing, sales, service, training, development, budgeting, and planning—that must be delivered consistently. As with resources, the number of processes employed by a company may be vast. But the important ones to focus on are those that are crucial to serving the CVP and profit formula. Although they are distinct elements of a successful business model and are the last to fully develop, I approach key resources and key processes in tandem. That's because the differentiation and sustainability of a successful business model depends on the unique way the key resources mesh with the key processes and how well they are knit together to repeatedly deliver the CVP and profit formula. In fact, the synergy between the key resources and key processes is as critical to the success of an enterprise as the key resources and processes are themselves.

Irish airline Ryanair's ability to provide a low-cost value proposition, for example, hinges on its related choices to service secondary airports, employ a nonunionized workforce, and ensure low overhead by, among other things, flying a standardized fleet of Boeing 737s and maintaining a spartan headquarters.[24] This potent combination of resources and processes work together harmoniously to support Ryanair's business model—a CVP of delivering radically discounted travel to customers through a profit formula reliant on high resource velocity and a low cost structure.

Medtronic's greatest asset is its depth of experience in making and marketing pacemakers and other medical devices

FIGURE 14

The Medtronic "Healthy Heart for All" business model

	Traditional manufacturer of pacemakers	Medtronic Healthy Heart for All
Customer value proposition	High-quality implantable cardiac pacemaker in developed markets covered by insurance	Solution to my cardiac disease made accessible through new channels and affordable through product innovation and third-party financing
Profit formula	High margins at scale, high overhead	Reduced margins at higher volumes through increased resource velocity and concurrent reduction in full-cost structure
Key resources and processes	• Best-in-class research and development • Superior manufacturing to ensure highest-quality products • Strong relationships with providers and payers	• Depth of experience making and marketing pacemakers worldwide • Strong relationships with the Indian medical community • Partnerships with third-party financiers

worldwide. It already had a strong presence in India and tremendous credibility with its medical community; being an established company, it had no trouble finding the partners that it needed in India's financial community.

Whole Foods owes much of its success to key process innovations that organized what had been an undeveloped and heterogeneous market. As noted earlier, the company originally relied heavily on supplies from small, local producers—mostly organic farmers and makers of naturopathic products. In the 1980s, there was no national market for these products or any centralized distributors or product aggregators on which to build a large-scale national operation. To deliver its game-changing CVP, Whole Foods had to build a supply-chain system unlike any that then existed in the grocery business.

Whole Foods grew partly by regional acquisitions, subsuming the existing store brands, but since local was a key component of its CVP, the company let local store managers continue to make

FIGURE 15

Whole Foods Market's business model

	Traditional mass-market grocer	Whole Foods Market
Customer value proposition	Broad range of store-brand, national, and premium-branded products; a time-efficient, self-serve experience	Convenient access to a broad range of foods and products that support environmentally and socially responsible practices; a pleasurable, high-touch shopping experience
Profit formula	Slim margins; emphasis on high-velocity dry goods and other items located in the center aisles	Higher margins; emphasis on produce, meats, prepared foods, and other fresh items located on the periphery
Key resources and processes	• Bargaining power with suppliers • Large-scale, centralized distribution network • Sourcing from national, regional, global networks • Standardized range of merchandise at all stores • Store designed to facilitate high volumes of purchases	• Relationships with local farmers and specialty merchants • Nine national distribution centers • Individual stores given autonomy to customize product mix, and stores individually organized from within • Stores designed to facilitate leisurely, social shopping experience

all the purchasing decisions, effectively decentralizing its supply-chain management.[25] As Whole Foods matured and its CVP became increasingly focused on high-quality perishables and prepared foods, it invested heavily in refining and systematizing this key process. It built discrete regional divisions and supplied them with its own national distribution network for specialty dry goods. To ensure high quality, it formed partnerships with local suppliers of organic perishables. Ultimately, the company shifted most of the purchasing and distribution responsibility for private label and nonperishable items to its own warehousing and distribution operations, but continued to allow regional and local managers to customize their product mix and stock directly from local producers.

Whole Foods innovated the traditional supermarket supply chain to serve its profit formula and achieved transformative
growth in its white space. As a result, it grew from a single store
staffed by nineteen people in 1980 to an effective manager of about
ten thousand suppliers, the bulk of them individuals or small, regional companies.[26] The decentralized nature of the business model
(and the key processes that fuel its success) enables individual stores
to operate as if they were independent business units but still enjoy
the benefits of being part of an extensive distribution network.

BUSINESS RULES, BEHAVIORAL NORMS, AND SUCCESS METRICS

Business rules, behavioral norms, and success metrics connect
the elements of a business model and keep the system in proper
balance. They ensure that the business can repeatedly and predictably deliver the CVP and fulfill the profit formula. Since
their function is to perpetuate the existing operations, they tend
to form last in the evolution of a business model. Over time, for
example, Whole Foods overlaid rules and metrics on its decentralized management chain to make sure that its various regions
adhered to the goals of its business model. Business rules and
behavioral norms guided its distributed decision-making network, and the company created a compensation system driven by
team metrics—not individual ones. Those controls helped Whole
Foods achieve consistency in its day-to-day operations, leading to
the greatest possible efficiencies and operating profits.

In the spring of 2017, Whole Foods Market was sold to the
retail sector's biggest disruptor, Amazon. Whether the internet
behemoth will preserve Whole Foods' existing business model or
change it to conform to its own remains to be seen.

Eventually, the elements of the business model fade into the
mists of institutional memory, even as it lives on as a practical

FIGURE 16

Rules, norms, and metrics

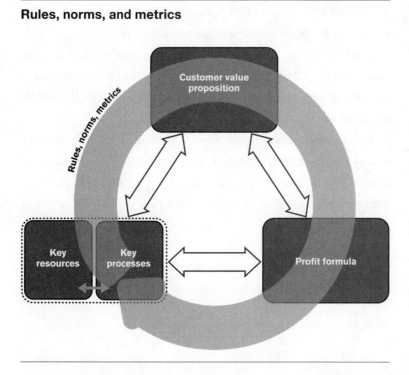

matter in the rules, cultural norms, and metrics. This institutional amnesia may explain why so many companies can operate so effectively without being able to articulate what their business model is. But since these guidelines and control mechanisms evolve precisely to optimize an existing business model, they severely inhibit the introduction of new business models, an important paradox that will be explored more fully in chapter 9.

A SOLID BLUEPRINT FOR INNOVATION

A company venturing into its white space without a clear framework for business model innovation is like a contractor trying to build a house with no blueprint to guide him. The contractor can generate a spreadsheet that shows that building a home would be profitable and then gather the resources needed to construct it, but when the lumber and concrete arrive at the site, the crew works aimlessly. Without a clear plan, any house that is built will probably look like the last house the crew worked on, because that's all they have to go on. If they do manage to create something original, it will have more to do with luck than with foresight.

The business model framework described in this chapter brings the discipline of architecture to business model innovation. With the blueprint it provides, you can diagram your existing core business model and design new models to help you seize your white space. The framework is the structure on which a manageable and more predictable innovation process can be built—a structure that can unlock your creativity as you pursue transformational growth and renewal.

Part Two

When New Business Models Are Needed

Any being, if it varies however slightly in any manner profitable to itself under the complex and varying conditions of life, will have a better chance of surviving, and thus be naturally selected.

—Charles Darwin

Imagine you are a Formula One race car driver. You have been racing an extremely sophisticated, fine-tuned machine on the streets of Monaco for years. You've applied breakthrough innovations in engine and suspension technology, radical new tire designs, and myriad other improvements to make your vehicle the best, most cutting-edge platform possible. You continually work to refine your strategies and tactics for winning races, and you have consistently collected the checks and trophies that victory brings. You've built a successful and profitable team, and few competitors can keep pace.

One day, however, you look to new horizons to grow as a competitor. The Baja 500 catches your interest, a challenging off-road race that traverses the Mexican desert. So you head to Baja, California, and start adjusting your Formula One machine to the task of barreling over rocks, sand washes, dry lake beds, and mountain passes. You narrow the wheelbase, install knobby tires, retool the transmission, upgrade the springs and shocks, and enhance the engine to make it run better in the hundred-plus-degree heat. Again, you study the course and develop a strategy. You're ready to compete when the starter flag falls.

You get dusted. No matter how many competitions you enter or how extensively you retool, your sophisticated Formula One machine simply cannot compete with rugged, kick-butt, off-road vehicles. All your experience, all your well-conceived strategies, and all your tactical prowess proves useless because your car is wrong for the Baja 500. If you want a shot at winning, you need a new racing platform.

So it is with business models. To compete and win a different type of race—to profitably satisfy a new job with a new customer value proposition in your white space—you need an entirely different business platform. You must reinvent your business model from top to bottom—changing all four elements and realigning how they interact.

Not all new CVPs require business model innovation; businesses can create game-changing new CVPs in new markets (and sometimes new industries) by taking advantage of the strength of their core model. These are adjacency moves. P&G, for example, has developed extremely innovative products within the context of its existing business model. Swiffer turned the common household mop from a commodity into a branded product and transformed the market in the process. Febreze created a new market category—cleaners for fabrics that are too large for the washer, like furniture and rugs—and then it was extended into unique air fresheners. Both Swiffer and Febreze innovatively satisfied new jobs-to-be-done, but P&G produces and distributes them according to its existing home-care business model, which is optimized to manufacture and distribute consumable products on a large scale.

How do you know if your new CVP requires a venture into your white space? You need a new model when, to fulfill the new customer value proposition, you find that you must take any of these steps:

- Change your current profit formula, especially the overhead cost structure, the resource velocity, or both.

- Develop many new kinds of key resources and processes.

- Create fundamentally different core metrics, rules, and norms to run your business.

When one or more of these conditions exists, the new opportunity lies in your white space, and you will need a new business model to compete.

Part 2 will help you gauge whether you can keep your Formula One race car or need to engineer a new dune buggy to tackle the next challenge. The following chapters will identify a range of market circumstances that present opportunities or imperatives for venturing into your white space through business model innovation and describe how certain companies did it successfully. Chapter 3 examines how business model innovation can help you address your white space within—opportunities to fulfill important but unsatisfied jobs-to-be-done for your existing customers within existing markets. Chapter 4 describes how you can use business model innovation to create new markets in your white space beyond. Here, the focus is on democratizing products and services, that is, making them accessible to large groups of potential consumers who have been shut out of a market entirely because existing offerings are too expensive, too complicated, or too time-consuming. Chapter 5 examines how the forces of industry transformation can create opportunities or imperatives that can be addressed through business model innovation in your white space between, the new terrain that emerges when some combination of transformative market shifts, innovative technology, or government policy creates massive industry upheaval. Finally, chapter 6 examines the ways that companies have turned new technologies into new opportunities for growth.

You should seek transformative growth and renewal proactively, but in a new race, you must first develop an eye for the most promising opportunities. These chapters will help you see them in new ways.

The White Space Within

Transforming Existing Markets

*The real voyage of discovery consists not in seeking
new landscapes but in having new eyes.*

—Marcel Proust

Dow **Corning began** its corporate life as a joint venture between
The Dow Chemical Company and Corning Glass Works to
investigate and commercialize silicone technology. It launched
its first product in 1943, a silicone compound that enabled
high-altitude flight by inhibiting moisture formation in aircraft
engines.[1] Fueled by the needs of World War II combat aircraft
and the boom in commercial air flight that followed, the company grew briskly and expanded into a wide variety of industries,
including construction, personal care, automotive, and medical
products. Through the years, Dow Corning's business model
powered a high-touch, solutions-oriented customer value proposition with an impressive array of more than seventy-five hundred product stock-keeping units, or SKUs.[2]

Then came disaster. In the 1990s, Dow Corning's silicone breast implants were implicated in various diseases, including breast cancer. Public outcry and massive class-action lawsuits led to a $3.2 billion settlement in 1998; the settlement drove the company to seek bankruptcy protection.[3] By 2001, Dow Corning faced a critical juncture. As a capital-intensive business, it found itself with significant excess manufacturing capacity and stagnating growth in many key product areas.

To address these challenges, the company hired a new CEO, Gary Anderson, who quickly replaced most of the company's senior management and began a massive restructuring. Anderson then tapped a well-regarded Dow Corning executive, Don Sheets, to build a small team to examine the company's existing customers. By gaining a better understanding of the customers' unfulfilled jobs-to-be-done, Anderson believed, Dow Corning would uncover new opportunities.

Sheets's team soon realized that many of Dow Corning's customers were in a mature phase. They were experienced in silicone applications, had been using the company's products for years, and knew exactly what they wanted. The company's silicone had virtually become a commodity. "If you look at our customer surveys over the years," says Sheets, "Dow Corning's customers' biggest concern was that our prices were too high. We were bundling our products and services together—R&D, product development, customer services—but a fairly large segment of customers just wanted to buy the product. They still wanted the same high-quality product and reliable supply, but they didn't want to pay for the services."[4]

With the web boom still echoing, Anderson suspected that there was an opportunity to create an internet-enabled business to address this growing market. So he gave Sheets a big title, a million dollars, and one year to figure it out. Sheets understood that the real challenge was to stimulate demand at the low end of the market—despite the fact that every part of Dow Corning's existing business model and culture functioned to deliver solutions for the high end. "The task wasn't to sell on the internet. I asked myself, rather, if there was a way to drive new demand into the company," Sheets says. "It quickly became pretty clear that to seize the opportunity, we would need a new business model."

Markets are born, grow, change, and die. Customer demand inevitably shifts, too, as do the jobs customers need to get done. To stay relevant, you must remain vigilant for these changes and devise new ways to address them. In the early stages of market development, these changes can often be successfully addressed by sustaining innovations—new products, services, or features— that fit well within your existing business model. At later stages, these shifts are often more profound and require you to reconsider your business model or develop a new one. When that happens, as it did for Dow Corning, you have the opportunity to seize your *white space within*: to achieve transformational growth or renewal within your existing market by delivering new CVPs, wrapped in appropriate business models, to address these new jobs-to-be-done.

THE SHIFTING BASIS OF COMPETITION

Opportunities within your white space often relate to predictable shifts in an industry's basis of competition—the aspects of an offering for which a customer is willing to pay a premium price.[5] Each shift emphasizes a different kind of innovation. At the early stage of market development, companies typically compete for customers on the basis of functionality. During this stage, customers will pay more for product features, functions, and value-added services that more closely fulfill the practical aspects of their jobs-to-be-done. Companies tend to go after these essential jobs first, and they build business models ideally suited to delivering continual product innovation. They compete by improving their products and services while reducing their costs and prices through greater efficiencies.

When these offerings reach a good-enough level and when performance-related jobs are mostly fulfilled, the basis of competition shifts. Customers will no longer pay a premium for additional performance improvements; they want higher quality and reliability. Because a product's functions and features become necessary but not sufficient to induce customers to buy, companies must differentiate their offerings by better satisfying customers' desires for well-made and reliable solutions. At that point, process innovation becomes the key to success. Companies refine their existing model to improve processes like procurement, manufacturing, customer relationship management, and technical support services, placing a special emphasis on quality assurance and quality control.

FIGURE 17

Shifts in the basis of competition

Companies compete on the basis of performance predominantly through product innovations. When the basis of competition moves to reliability, they tend to respond through process innovations. But once the basis shifts to convenience and cost, business model innovation often comes into play as well.

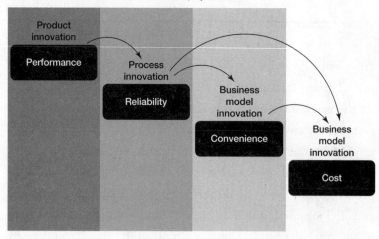

When Japanese automakers entered the US market in the 1960s, for example, they introduced small cars like the Toyota Corona to establish a foothold with price-sensitive buyers. In the late 1970s and early 1980s, however, they shifted the basis of competition by producing cars of significantly higher quality. Doing so didn't require a whole new business model; the automakers made process improvements to key business functions like manufacturing and vendor management. Customers were happy to spend more for high-quality, reliable cars, and their willingness to pay helped Japanese automakers move upmarket to serve the middle and high-end tiers of car consumers.

Once most of the functionality and reliability requirements of consumers are met, the basis of competition shifts yet again. Customers begin to demand innovations that allow them to fulfill their jobs-to-be-done more quickly, more easily, or in a way more precisely tailored to their individual needs. Companies now compete through convenience and customization to garner premium prices. Companies like Zipcar and Car2Go, for example, compete directly on convenience. Customers who want to use a car but don't want to own one outright (perhaps to reduce their carbon footprint or simply to avoid the hassles of city parking) have happily signed on for car-sharing services, which fulfill many of the jobs of car ownership with fewer of its drawbacks.

Finally, when a competitive offering accomplishes most jobs related to all three aspects of performance—reliability, convenience, and cost—the market becomes essentially commoditized. At that point, companies compete almost solely on cost. The progression is not always linear; the basis of competition can shift directly from reliability to cost. That often occurs in business-to-business companies and in industries that are driven by technological advances like steel manufacturing and chemicals, as well as for original equipment manufacturers (OEMs) like makers of computer disk drives.

When the basis of competition and a customer's priority jobs-to-be-done change, the required CVP fundamentally changes as well. This is when companies most often find themselves at the limits of their existing business models. To deliver value propositions that satisfy these new jobs and take advantage of the new opportunities for growth they represent, companies must embark on business model innovation, as Dow Corning discovered.

DOW CORNING: THE ALCHEMY OF CHANGE

When many incumbents come up against the forces of full-on commoditization, they cede the low end of the market to their competitors and chase higher margins at the top by clinging to their core business model. But that approach can seriously harm their long-term prospects. Dow Corning's Don Sheets thought there might be a better way. Focusing on customer jobs, he recognized that if the company wanted to grow, it would have to radically change the way it competed.

Sheets gathered his small team and began to formulate a CVP that would fulfill the job-to-be-done of price-driven customers. The team targeted a price point 15 percent lower than current offerings.[6] This was an ambitious goal—not only because 15 percent represents a huge reduction in commodity pricing, but also because Dow Corning had a high-margin culture. Sheets knew that to build a business with any chance of success, his team would have to create a business model that would lower costs while still delivering the kinds of margins that the company's finance people would accept.

Merely eliminating services would not do it. A 15 percent price reduction called for a profit formula that combined a dramatically lower cost structure with much higher resource velocity. So the team devised ways to remove inventory costs by limiting the range of allowable lead times and by manufacturing products only after an order was received. They increased velocity by selling and shipping in larger units, allowing far less variation in the size of orders and eliminating value-added services, thus moving more silicone through the system faster. Breaking away from Dow Corning's traditional high-touch customized approach, the new venture needed to automate and standardize offerings to reduce overhead and the number of people involved in each transaction. That change called for a new key resource—a strong IT backbone that could automate the value chain and enable much of the business to be conducted online. This shift toward automation would have to be reflected in new business rules, which would need to be stricter than Dow Corning's old rules. For example, order sizes would be limited to a few large-volume options; order lead times would be between two and four weeks; credit terms would be fixed; and rates for silicone would be set on the spot market rather than negotiated case by case. Customers that wanted exceptions to these rules would have to pay more.

As the vision for this new venture sharpened, the team realized how radical it was. Low-touch, self-service, and standardized, the new business was almost diametrically opposed to the model that governed Dow Corning's core operating space.

Seeing how different the new business would be, Sheets set out to determine if it could succeed within the confines of Dow Corning's core enterprise. He set up a war game to test the reactions of existing staff and systems to these strict new business rules. The new model got crushed; it was just too foreign to Dow Corning's current modes of working. The way forward became clear. If it was going to thrive, the new venture would have to be free from the core business model. To protect and nurture the opportunity, Dow Corning needed a new company with a unique identity. It launched Xiameter to seize its white space.

Following the explicit articulation of the new CVP and profit formula, Xiameter focused on implementing and integrating the

FIGURE 18

Dow Corning and Xiameter's different business models

	Dow Corning	Xiameter
Customer value proposition	Customized solutions, negotiated contracts	No frills, bulk prices, sold through the internet
Profit formula	Negotiated prices, high overhead, high margin	Spot-market pricing, low overhead, lower margins, high throughput
Key resources and processes	• R&D • Sales • Service orientation	• IT system • Lowest-cost processes • Maximum automation

key resources and key processes it would need to succeed. Information technology, a small part of Dow Corning's core competencies, would be an essential piece of the new internet-based business, so a small team quickly built a fully automated, web-based order and delivery system. Xiameter's brand image also required careful attention: it needed to be connected to Dow Corning but sufficiently separate for customers to understand that this was not their father's silicone company. Sheets settled on pairing the name Xiameter with a tagline that read "The new measure of value. From Dow Corning," to emphasize both strengths.

Xiameter recognized that its people would be a key resource, but the need for low overhead kept staff size small. Some employees would have to act decisively in a fast-changing market, a behavioral norm not critical to Dow's core operations. "Xiameter was going to be about making fast decisions," says Sheets. "Most of the organization was going to be traders on the front lines, making decisions about where to set prices according to the spot market, and there were going to be big implications for those decisions. I needed people who could make good decisions quickly—those who would thrive in a fast-changing environment filled with a lot of ambiguity."

To import expertise from the parent company without importing the mindset of the core, Sheets searched to identify Dow Corning staffers who, while they were team players, didn't quite fit into its culture. "We were looking for expert people who really knew their markets," he says. But Sheets also wanted "willing-to-stick-their-necks-out people." During interviews, when he found likely candidates, he asked them to take the new job on the spot. That allowed him to gauge how comfortable they were with making quick decisions. "This was exactly the right attitude I was looking for," says Sheets. "A different caliber of people than the traditional Dow Corning salesperson, for sure."

Having articulated a clear CVP, constructed an appropriate profit formula, and put the key resources and processes in place, Xiameter needed institutional patience and protection to allow it to find its way. Dow Corning, for its part, wanted to control development costs and make sure reasonable accountability metrics were put in place. So Xiameter developed an aggressive timetable for launch but deliberately kept the scale of the operation small so that team members could learn as they went. "Milestones were critical," says Sheets. "We set deadlines and worked feverishly toward them. This fast-paced environment allowed us to show early results while simultaneously developing a unique mini-culture within Xiameter."

As Xiameter took off, it began to deliver unexpected benefits to Dow Corning as a whole. Xiameter's lower prices enabled Dow Corning to utilize its substantial excess manufacturing capacity profitably. Over time, new customers helped fill industry capacity, driving up prices overall and increasing profitability in the core. Because Xiameter's model allowed it to capitalize on opportunities in times of market instability—changing its prices every hour if it chose to—the new company could respond to fluctuations in raw material and energy costs much faster than Dow Corning could. This flexibility also raised profits.

Xiameter paid back Dow Corning's investment in just three months and went on to become a major transformative success. Before it launched Xiameter, Dow Corning had no online sales component. By 2006, roughly 35 percent of its sales originated online—nearly three times the industry average.[7]

Although Xiameter began with existing customers, many are now new to the company—those that previously couldn't afford Dow Corning products. According to Sheets, "When Xiameter started pouring orders into our manufacturing facilities, people woke up. This was not just some web thing; this was affecting real people, real manufacturing operations, real profits. And that was awesome."

As Dow Corning learned, when crossing the competitive threshold to a fully commoditized state, business models often need to be reexamined. To compete at the low end, a company must typically redefine its profit formula, key resources, and key processes to lower costs through greater automation, and this often means stricter business rules that reduce variability and standardize offerings.

Dow Corning recognized the shift in the job-to-be-done of some of its existing customers early, before it could be disrupted by competitors or new entrants. By embracing business model innovation and building a model ideally suited to serving these new jobs, the company seized its white space and created a powerful new engine of transformational growth.

Looking back a decade later, that growth path, though steady, has not been altogether smooth. In a premature expansion effort, Xiameter departed from the market segmentation principles it had established and added hundreds of other products from Dow Corning's core business, thereby changing a key piece of its business model. It also aggressively pushed out into the developing world, where customers had less familiarity with some of the products and would have benefited from Dow Corning's traditional customized-sales approach. Though Dow Corning continued to increase its online revenue, it lost overall market share. "We stopped asking the customers how they want to buy," Dan Futter, Dow Corning's senior vice president of sales and customer experience, told us in a 2017 interview, "and got fascinated with the fact that [online sales] take a lot of cost out for us. We moved into newer materials . . . and got besotted with how we wanted to sell."

Dow Corning was wholly acquired by The Dow Chemical Company in June 2016, and Xiameter is now poised for its biggest expansion yet, as it prepares to introduce a no-frills, web-order platform for all Dow Chemical brands. Xiameter will no longer be synonymous with silicone, but will get ahead with its business model—one that has yet to be successfully replicated in its industry. Xiameter's key strength, Futter noted, remains its real-time inventory system and instant auto-confirmation. "The big breakdown for most players," he told us, "is that you need a perfect alignment between your ERP [enterprise resource planning] and your web interface. How those things interact has to be a direct representation of your business model." For customers who know precisely what they want and when they need it, the Xiameter platform perfectly satisfies their job-to-be-done.

COMPETING ON CONVENIENCE

Competing head-on with a new customer value proposition targeted at the low end of the market is one response to commoditization. Sometimes companies can sidestep the rush to the bottom and instead shift the basis of competition from reliability to convenience and customization. Doing so will often require them to stop concentrating solely on product or process innovations and consider more multifaceted ways to deliver value. Product manufacturers, for instance, may need to add an educational component to a previously successful product or adopt a more flexible manufacturing process to meet the needs of increasingly demanding customers.

In the early days of the PC industry, for example, companies like Apple, Compaq, IBM, and Tandy addressed functional jobs in the market, and their innovations focused on product improvements. Apple became an early leader because its well-integrated products satisfied the performance needs of the market better than its competitors' offerings did. Its products were more reliable (they crashed far less often) and much easier to use. Other companies played catch-up, innovating both products and processes to deliver better-performing and more-reliable computers. Then Dell Computer Corporation changed everything.

Dell computers were not initially as good as those of the established PC manufacturers, but Dell wasn't competing on the features and functionality of its products, which were already good enough in the eyes of most consumers. Instead, it introduced a new level of customization and convenience to the PC industry. Dell's unique business model allowed customers to pick up the phone (and, later, log on to a website) and order exactly the computer they wanted, preloaded with exactly the software they needed, delivered to their door almost overnight. This new business model—from its offering (customized product, direct sales, and forty-eight-hour delivery) to the way its products were sourced and assembled (just-in-time supply chain)—was nothing like the way PCs had been made and sold. Dell forcibly shifted the basis of competition to convenience and customization. Thirty years later, with not just prices and margins but demand for PCs reaching historic lows, it remains to be seen whether Dell, once the innovator, can reinvent its business model to address a new CVP.

New product innovations aimed at functionality and quality jobs do not sustain themselves as long as they once did. More entrants compete on the basis of convenience sooner, and as a result, markets move to total commoditization faster than they did in the past. Dow Corning's silicone business and Dell's PC business took decades to shift toward full commoditization; for newer industries, the time frame is shrinking. Still, our new Convenience Era brings not only threats but also opportunities. Faced with the maturation of its power-tool market, the Liechtenstein-based toolmaker Hilti learned that threats and opportunities could sometimes be indistinguishable.

HILTI: DRILLING DOWN ON BUSINESS MODEL INNOVATION

Compared with the extremely large and complex machines produced by firms like Caterpillar, the handheld power tools Hilti makes are simple and inexpensive. While large-equipment costs can run into the millions of dollars, a reasonably sized construction site would typically contain only about $20,000 worth of Hilti's products. In each small tool, however, lie great opportunity costs: a malfunctioning or broken item can halt construction for a day or more, costing exorbitant sums in lost productivity and delayed time lines.

In the late 1990s, Hilti realized that its market was commoditizing. Many of its product technologies were overshooting customer expectations; further incremental improvements were not only failing to drive growth but also failing to halt their declining market share. "We found ourselves losing ground to competitors in the small-tool market," says Marco Meyrat, executive board member and head of sales and marketing for Europe and North America. "We are a premium brand, and in that segment, premium was of less value. Differentiation was harder for us to attain."[8] But Hilti wasn't prepared to cede the market, so, like Dow Corning, it turned to its customers to determine its next move.

During this process, Hilti identified a side effect of power-tool commoditization: construction workers viewed these tools as virtually disposable. They often left them out in the rain, maintained them poorly, or forgot them at the site. Neglect decreased productivity and increased repair costs for companies already struggling with thinning margins. At the same time, the profusion of cheap battery-powered hand tools left worksite tool tables scattered with mismatched components from different manufacturers. Maintaining and transporting tools was burdensome to customers, and it was becoming a growing challenge for construction sites to manage their "fleet" of tools over the course of a project. "Tool management is a pain," says Hilti's chair and former CEO, Pius Baschera. "A construction crew's purpose is to build a house, not manage tools."[9] Predicting which tools, and how many of each, would be needed on a given day was complex. For big customers, process costs were becoming even more of a headache than repair costs; the added hassle of trying to organize and account for tools taxed already-strained resources. In short, though hand tools themselves were commoditizing, managing them had become difficult, and that represented a higher cost.

By examining the jobs-to-be-done of its customers, Hilti saw that commoditization—its dreaded enemy—had actually created an opportunity to change the game in the power-tool industry by competing on convenience and customization. Recognizing the way its customers were using (and abusing) its products, Meyrat and his team conceived of a leasing model for fleets of tools. Instead of buying power tools individually and dealing with their upkeep and management on their own, customers could pay a monthly fee to have a full complement of tools at their fingertips, well-inventoried, in full repair, and insured against theft. "The value proposition for the customer was basically, 'We take care of everything, and he always has the newest technology and the safest tools, well organized and readily available,'" says Meyrat.

Though the new business seemed logical and built on what looked at first blush to be Hilti's core expertise, this leasing model represented a fundamentally new CVP, and Hilti's profit formula would have to adjust accordingly. "Clearly, it was a complete change in how we looked at revenue," Meyrat observes. "The customer no longer pays up front by buying the tool. He gets and uses the tool, and we get the money month by month." What's more, Hilti could no longer move inventory off its balance sheet every month; it would have to become a service business, both leasing tangible assets and providing new forms of intangible services. Sales transactions would be fewer but much larger. Margins would be higher, but so would overhead and administrative costs. In short, to meet the unserved jobs of its customers, Hilti would have to venture far from the safe confines of its core manufacturing and sales business to compete in its white space within.

Because this new CVP had come directly from its existing customers and because many of the tool-related elements of the model were familiar, Hilti was able to quickly design a rudimentary blueprint for its offering and profit formula. Then it began to work out the key resources and key processes it would need. Contract management was its first priority. Customers would want the flexibility to add or remove individual tools from their contracts at any time. Because the new CVP was all about reducing customers' administrative costs, Hilti would have to maintain these complex contracts itself, an intense backroom capability that it would have to build from the ground up. To be profitable, Hilti would need to keep these costs low and be very disciplined with its customers about contractual add-ons. Additionally, the company had to devise a process to manage and maintain fleets of tools more inexpensively and effectively than its customers had. And it required a constant supply of fresh tools that could immediately replace ones that broke.

On the customer management side, Hilti needed to develop a website that would allow construction managers to view all the tools in their fleets (or several fleets at different sites) to monitor their usage rates. This data would help managers conveniently handle the cost accounting associated with these assets.

Meyrat says, however, that the greatest key-resource challenge Hilti faced was training its sales force to do a thoroughly new task. Fleet management is not a half-hour sale; it takes days, weeks, even months of meetings to convince customers to change their behavior and buy a program instead of a product. "This was not spot selling, which is what we mostly did, but rather going into partnership with customers over a number of years," he explained. Suddenly, field reps accustomed to dealing with crew leaders and purchasing managers in mobile trailers on site found themselves sitting across a conference table from CEOs and CFOs, since typically only an executive can sign off on such a program. The reps needed to wear suits, not work clothes. "Our salespeople confessed that they didn't have the courage to go up to the C-suite," says Meyrat. So Hilti

FIGURE 19

The Hilti business model

	Traditional power-tool company	Tool fleet management services
Customer value proposition	Industrial and professional power tools and accessories	Comprehensive tool fleet management service to increase on-site productivity
Profit formula	Low margins, high inventory turnover	Higher margins; asset-heavy (tool leasing); monthly payments for tool maintenance, repair, and replacement
Key resources and processes	• Distribution channel • Low-cost manufacturing plants in developing countries • R&D	• Strong direct-sales approach • Contract management • IT systems for inventory management and repair • Warehousing

committed significant resources to helping its staff overcome those cultural barriers.

To test its assumptions and develop the model, Hilti kept the initiative small at first, establishing a foothold market to prove— and improve—the proposition and thoroughly work out all the new key resources and processes the business model required. "We started in Switzerland, which we consider a home country, where we have strong brand position, deep customer relationships, a high-quality customer base, and a stable currency," explains Meyrat. Hilti began the new business with just eight customers, and the results were immediately encouraging. "When I looked at the share of wallet we were getting and their behavior," Meyrat recalls, "I saw they were not only giving us their tools but a larger share of their consumables budget. When I started to extrapolate the numbers for these few customers, they were almost magic in terms of what was possible."

Seeing profit early, Hilti could afford to be patient for growth as it continued to develop the right combination of contract management and accounting rules and metrics to allow the business to scale up. Initially, for instance, Hilti stipulated that it would present this option only to large customers. But it quickly learned that small and medium-sized construction firms that used as few as fifty Hilti tools also found the proposition attractive, albeit for different reasons. To them, unexpected costs of repair and replacement had a big impact on the bottom line, and scaling up for peak loads presented serious financial challenges. The new offering enabled these smaller customers not only to hedge against the downsides but also to scale more nimbly and efficiently in upturns.

Hilti piloted the program in 2000 and, within three years, rolled it out throughout most of the worldwide markets in which it operated. The program has grown steadily: by 2015, Hilti's Fleet Management Division was managing more than a million tools for one hundred thousand customers around the world, accounting for a significant part of Hilti's tools and overall sales revenue of $4.2 billion.

FULFILLING UNSERVED JOBS IN EXISTING MARKETS

Shifts in the basis of competition may create an imperative to venture into your white space within through business model innovation. But opportunities can arise whenever customers have jobs-to-be-done that are not fulfilled by existing CVPs. FedEx, for example, used a jobs-based focus to introduce a new business model to the package-delivery industry even though the industry was not shifting.

As an undergraduate at Yale, founder Fred Smith flew charter planes out of Tweed New Haven Airport in Connecticut to make some extra money. At the small northeastern airports he frequented, he noticed that many of the corporate jets belonging to the rising powerhouses of the electronic age, companies like IBM and Xerox, were being used to transport high-priced components to field service engineers who were repairing computers. People needed these expensive parts, and they needed them right away; speed was clearly more important than cost. One company— Emery Air Freight—was trying to address this job, but it had built its infrastructure around passenger airlines serving large cities. At that time, the aviation industry was heavily regulated, and airlines flew mostly point-to-point routes, so reaching smaller cities was difficult. Emery was "force-fitting the rapid movement of high-value-added and high-technology products into a transportation system that wasn't designed for it," Smith explains.[10]

Seeing an opportunity, Smith envisioned a fundamentally different business model uniquely designed to serve a single unaddressed job-to-be-done: reliably move valuable packages from point A to point B overnight. He bought a small aviation company and, to fulfill that job, created an integrated air and land system based on the then-revolutionary hub-and-spoke approach. Smith's company blew Emery out of the market. Beginning in 1971 from a humble fleet of fourteen small aircraft serving twenty-five US cities, Federal Express became in 1983 the first US company ever to book $1 billion in revenue without a merger or an acquisition.[11]

High-end overnight delivery remained a niche market until government deregulation of airfreight opened it to letter and document transport. Vast numbers of consumers wanted to send documents and other packages reliably from city to city overnight, and they, too, were willing to pay a premium to do it. FedEx's business model was uniquely suited to satisfy that need. The US Postal Service and UPS had held government-protected near monopolies in this market, and neither was prepared to respond to the new entrant. (Although overnight package delivery might seem to be a natural extension of UPS's core efforts, the company's business model focused on ground transportation, relied on existing air routes and carriers, and couldn't initially deliver the speed or reliability the market wanted.) It took UPS and the US Postal Service years to transform their business models to catch up.

Furniture maker IKEA is another example of a newcomer that transformed an existing market, in this case by creating a unique business model that addressed the job-to-be-done of young couples who wanted low-cost but fashion-forward furniture. The idea was transformative because it was not merely about lowering the cost of furniture (which many discount houses already were doing). What IKEA did was turn furniture from a durable into a nondurable good. High-quality, big-ticket furniture is a high-stakes purchase because people have to keep it for a long time to get their investment back. Buying IKEA's furniture is more akin to buying clothing—something its young customers could do over and over again as they moved from apartment to starter house to larger house, or just grew out of their adolescent taste.

That's why the furniture needed to be both radically less expensive than the high-end alternatives but also far trendier than the discount offerings.

To further cement the value proposition, IKEA combined the shopping experience of a showroom with the convenience of a logistics facility: after seeing the furniture staged in hip, stylish rooms, customers purchased their selections in modular and easily transportable kits, which they could take home the same day and assemble themselves. All of IKEA's products and services (in-store childcare, heavily discounted food) are backed up by a profit formula and key resources and processes that are uniquely integrated to deliver its CVP.

Similarly, as we saw in chapter 2, Whole Foods Market built an integrated business model that satisfied the unserved jobs-to-be-done for its high-end customers. In all three cases—FedEx, IKEA, and Whole Foods—incumbents were slow to recognize and largely unable to respond to the unique nature of these new business models, which were aimed squarely at their white space within. It can be argued that it's easier for startups to capitalize on such opportunities, since incumbents are hampered by the imperatives of their existing business models, a problem startups simply don't have. But that needn't be the case: whether newly emerged from shifts in the basis of competition or lurking unrecognized within a market, unserved jobs-to-be-done present powerful opportunities for transformational growth and renewal to incumbent companies as well, through business model innovation.

The White Space Beyond

Creating New Markets

*One does not discover new lands without consenting
to lose sight of the shore for a very long time.*

—André Gide

India is home to 16 percent of the world's population. It is also home to 28 percent of the world's hair, which is a very good statistic if you happen to sell shampoo.[1] Hindustan Unilever took advantage of these statistics to nearly triple its sales and profits between 2004 and 2009.[2]

The company had been a market leader in personal care products for years, initially finding success among India's rising middle class and then introducing a wide range of brands appealing to low-income market segments. Leadership in such a rapidly developing market might seem to guarantee a long run of growth. But thanks to shrinking profit margins and increased competition, by the end of the twentieth century, Hindustan

Unilever needed to find new markets and new growth, according to Nitin Paranjpe, who became CEO of Hindustan Unilever in 2008 (he is president of Unilever Home Care today).

That would not be easy. India had an average annual income of just $600; large swaths of its inhabitants lived in poverty. But Hindustan Unilever's leadership was determined, and in 1999, the company formed a task force of middle managers, Paranjpe among them. "We were charged with finding new ideas and new models to help the organization," he says.[3]

Meanwhile, dramatic changes were afoot in Indian society. The once tightly controlled economy was liberalizing quickly, and the government had begun a wide-scale effort to improve the quality of life in rural India. "India lives in its villages," the saying goes. At the turn of the millennium, 72 percent of India's 1.13 billion people lived in the countryside (the percentage is about 67 percent today).[4] Most of those 600,000-plus villages are remote, and their roads can't handle large shipments of goods or much commerce above a subsistence economy. Rather than invest in expensive infrastructure, India's government chose to support the creation of self-help groups composed predominantly of women. The idea was to help rural entrepreneurs start businesses and so improve living conditions in their regions.

Hindustan Unilever looked at this changing social dynamic and saw a white space that it could capitalize on. "Rural India was approaching an inflection point," says Paranjpe. "The challenge was to turn it into an opportunity."[5]

DEMOCRATIZING PRODUCTS AND SERVICES

While business model innovation provides you with a powerful process to exploit the white space within your existing markets, it is equally effective in unlocking even more exciting opportunities to serve entirely new customers and create new markets—to seize your *white space beyond*. Seizing your white space beyond means developing new business models in support of customer value propositions aimed at potential customers who are currently nonconsumers. Nonconsumption occurs when large groups of potential customers are shut out of a market because existing offerings are too expensive, too complicated, or inaccessible.

To open up new markets and address their jobs-to-be-done, a company must first determine what factors prevent those jobs from being met and, more fundamentally, what barriers constrain consumption by those underserved customers. There are four main barriers to consumption: skills, access, time, and wealth.[6] Software maker Intuit devised the accounting software QuickBooks to fulfill the job of many small-business owners: "Help me not run out of cash." The software broke the skills barrier that excluded these owners from more sophisticated and complicated offerings like Peachtree. Whole Foods Market helped relatively wealthy consumers break the access barrier by organizing the chaotic natural-foods and organic-produce markets into one rational, locally available supply chain. And Minnesota-based MinuteClinic (now owned by CVS) broke the time barrier to health care by putting nurse practitioners in drugstore kiosks to provide treatment for simple medical ailments without appointments and within about thirty minutes.

Nonconsumers fall all along the socioeconomic spectrum, although opportunities to democratize products in emerging markets and reach the so-called bottom of the pyramid are particularly ripe. As the global economy fuels upward mobility for even the poorest in developing nations, many companies are finding growth by breaking down barriers for consumers they previously thought to be unreachable, unprofitable, or both.

For example, the infrastructure costs involved in delivering telecommunications services to remote rural areas once made such services unfeasible in developing countries. Now cellular technology—distributed through a leasing model by companies like América Móvil and Vodafone—has changed that dynamic. In the 1990s, Chinese appliance maker Galanz began manufacturing small, energy-efficient microwave ovens that could be used in cramped Chinese apartments with limited power supplies. With a business model that was profitable at domestic Chinese price points, Galanz opened up a vast market of former nonconsumers and went on to capture nearly 40 percent of the world market.[7] The South African bank Absa created an innovative franchise model for a profitable microlending division that promoted economic development in townships while also recruiting nonconsumers into the financial services sector.

"We're living in an era where the technologies that have empowered high living standards and 80-year life expectancies in the rich world are now for almost everybody," notes economist Jeffrey Sachs, director of Columbia University's Earth Institute. "Not only do we have a very large amount of economic activity right now, but we have pent-up potential for vast increases [in economic activity] as well."[8] Recognizing this enormous potential in the remote villages of rural India, Hindustan Unilever acted to seize its white space.

THE SHAKTI INITIATIVE

When Hindustan Unilever started its search for new opportunities, it set up a task force with a clear mission: devise a model that could break the wealth and access barriers that kept hundreds of millions of nonconsumers from the market. And do so in a way that would improve lives—do well by doing good, as the company came to think of it. Inspired by the microfinance model of Grameen Bank, started by Muhammad Yunus in Bangladesh, the task force began to envision a business model centered on partnerships with those government-supported, microcredit-financed village self-help groups. The venture, called the Shakti Initiative, would reach out to those embryonic entrepreneurs, identifying and training a sales force termed the *Shakti ammas* ("strength mothers"). These women would act as direct representatives for Hindustan Unilever in their villages. For the company, it was a radical idea on many levels. "First, we had to break the mindset that said it was not viable to go directly to a village with two thousand people in it," noted Govind Rajan, then Hindustan Unilever's general manager and category head of skin care. "Then we realized that we could give something back to society on a large scale in a mutually beneficial manner."[9]

To build a partner network, Hindustan Unilever needed to reconceive its approach to distribution. "We always saw distribution as something we did," Rajan said. "We never thought about a direct-to-consumer approach. We went in, serviced the dealers, and got out. As we went along with Shakti, we learned about connecting and partnering. This was the first time we ventured into managing businesses at a micro scale."[10]

To work closely with rural self-help groups, microcredit lenders, nongovernmental organizations (NGOs), and the Indian government—the forces that were changing the nature of the market—required new skills and new processes. "It is an entirely different mindset to work with people who are not P&L oriented," Rajan said. "Their passion is for society and how people feel about themselves."[11]

Knowing it needed to build an appropriate platform, the team worked hard to clearly define the target customer. Ultimately, members arrived at a surprising CVP: Shakti was not really about delivering products to the end user; it was about delivering a business opportunity to the Shakti ammas, who were the true new customers. "Delivering a business opportunity became the white space play," Paranjpe noted. "We focused on the channel, delivering adequate training and support to ensure their profitability. We would only succeed if every member of the channel succeeded as well."[12]

By defining the direct representative as the customer and focusing the value proposition on giving her a viable business opportunity, Hindustan Unilever built a model designed for long-term growth—a model that was difficult for competitors to replicate. Although rival Nirma, an Indian consumer- and industrial-products company, had beaten Hindustan Unilever to the direct-sales approach, Hindustan Unilever hoped its unique focus on a partner network model would give it an infrastructure and expertise that differentiated the company in the rural market. Early on, Shakti team members realized that the profit formula for this new model would have to tolerate low margins as the offerings gained a foothold in communities unaccustomed to purchasing branded products.[13] They expected those margins to be balanced by increased volume, and they also included the social benefit of the enterprise in their metrics for success, a position supported by Hindustan Unilever's corporate leadership. To test the assumptions underlying the Shakti model, Hindustan Unilever started in only one region. Just seventeen women began selling hand soap, shampoo, and a small list of other products in their village market and then went increasingly door to door.[14]

Since the CVP was to serve the channel, Shakti needed to provide sales training and business support for the ammas—new key resources—to help them understand the brand and to run a profitable small business.

"This was not a typical customer development project that could be executed through traditional MBA skills," said Krishnendu Dasgupta, the team's channel manager. "We needed new skills and a different mindset."[15] These women had varying levels of education, so Hindustan Unilever couldn't simply hand them routine training manuals. Instead, the Shakti team created training audiocassettes and invited the women to attend classroom programs in the nearest locations.[16] Because advertising and marketing were also unfamiliar concepts, the Shakti team sometimes hired troupes of local actors to travel from village to village performing comedic skits—a live commercial extolling brand messages.[17]

Many of those messages focused on the benefits of increased hygiene. Teaching a rural population the benefits of washing hands before eating—thus decreasing intestinal infections, a leading cause of childhood mortality—made the ammas more than Avon representatives; it gave them increased social stature because they provided an important benefit to the village.

"We wanted to improve the quality of life, but it also had to be profitable," said Sanjiv Kakkar, now the chair of Unilever Russia, Ukraine, and Belarus.[18] The team's efforts paid off right from the start. The average Shakti entrepreneur brought in enough money to effectively double her household income, and the impact on the community was palpable. "Every time I visited a Shakti family, I could see the happiness in their faces," said Dasgupta. "Shakti changes lives. People have touched my feet, an honor normally reserved for elders only."[19]

But challenges remained. Getting product to remote villages required further innovation in distribution. Many of the target markets lacked paved roads. At first, Shakti leveraged Hindustan Unilever's existing rural distribution network, arranging drop-off points for the ammas to pick up their weekly deliveries, which they often would transport to their villages on carts towed by bicycles. As it incubated the model, however, the team found that it was more efficient to develop entrepreneurs in geographic clusters. By reducing the number of drop-off points, local distributors made higher profits, and Shakti could decrease stock requirements, which in turn increased efficiency and resource velocity.[20] As the Shakti team honed the profit formula and refined the key resources and processes to nail the job-to-be-done, operations expanded to sixty women by the beginning of 2003 and then to twenty-eight hundred women entrepreneurs covering twelve thousand villages by the end of that year.[21] To protect growth, the core team stayed focused on its CVP of delivering a powerful business opportunity. "Our metrics were all about establishing viability," said Paranjpe, "not sales volume. We wanted to put as little pressure on the distribution stream as possible until we proved its viability." Accordingly, the Shakti team rigorously analyzed all the elements of its business model, carefully considering the cost of each, watching for possible cannibalization of Hindustan Unilever's existing rural streams, and adjusting the model at every step. "Only when we understood how the model could work did we start to scale up," said Paranjpe.[22]

The Shakti Initiative lost money for the first three years, during the investment phase, as the model was established. Extrapolating from the early profitability of the Shakti ammas' efforts, however, the team clearly saw that overall profit would soon follow scale. "This kept us from being overanxious for growth," Paranjpe noted.[23]

By 2007, the model had been refined and tested extensively. It was time to ramp up the business. Shakti expanded to forty-five thousand Shakti ammas covering more than one hundred thousand villages across fifteen states, reaching over three million homes.[24] In 2008, the Shakti ammas bought the equivalent of almost $100 million worth of consumer goods from Hindustan Unilever.[25]

Thus, Shakti became an engine of transformational growth for Hindustan Unilever, dramatically increasing its rural penetration and adding new perspectives, capabilities, and expertise to the parent company. "Shakti occupies a very special place in my heart," Dasgupta concluded. "I wake up every morning and go to work at Hindustan Unilever knowing that I am contributing to society and improving the lives of thousands of underprivileged

FIGURE 20

Hindustan Unilever and the Shakti Initiative

	Traditional consumer packaged goods business	Hindustan Unilever Shakti Initiative
Customer value proposition	Retailer is the customer. Distributes product through established third parties in concentrated population centers	Shakti amma woman is the customer. Deliver not just a product but a business opportunity to Shakti ammas, who represent and sell products in their villages. "Do good while making a profit."
Profit formula	Low per-unit cost; economies of scale; large inventory	Initially lower margins but much greater quantity; high trade margins on low-per-unit-cost products
Key resources and processes	Distribution as an internally focused process	Distribution through: • Partner network • Training and distribution systems • Creative direct marketing • New brand message (focused on health)

people. It makes me very proud."[26] Today, with more than seventy thousand representatives serving more than four million households in India, Shakti's partner network model is a platform for Hindustan Unilever's next stage of growth, and the company is working to replicate the model.[27] Similar initiatives are under way in Southeast Asia, Africa, and Latin America, democratizing offerings for millions more nonconsumers and unlocking vast new markets.

DEMOCRATIZING KNOWLEDGE AND UNDERSTANDING

Chapter 3 discussed how shifts in the basis of competition can create opportunities within your market. Shifts in knowledge can do this too.

Like the bases of competition, the ways we solve problems also change over time. When we know very little about a problem, we tend to guess a lot, and when we know a lot, we tend to follow well-known patterns or specific rules to find solutions. These differences in approaches are known as the *problem-solving continuum*. As the problem-solving ability within an industry progresses along this spectrum, white-space opportunities open up, allowing you to develop new CVPs and new business models that democratize products and services and overcome barriers to consumption.[28]

To illustrate how shifts along the problem-solving continuum can create new opportunities, let's look at the challenge of determining if a woman is pregnant. Before the advent of modern medicine, people simply guessed, stumbling around in the metaphorical dark for some clear indicator that a baby was on its way. The ancient Egyptians wet bags of wheat and barley with the urine of a possibly pregnant woman; if the grain germinated, they believed the woman was pregnant. Hippocrates suggested that a woman drink honey water at bedtime; if she suffered abdominal distention and cramps, he postulated that she was pregnant. Through the nineteenth century, the most reliable method was the careful observation of a woman's own physical symptoms, such as morning sickness or the fact that she missed her menstrual period for several months.[29]

Around 1927, however, doctors discovered that the urine of a pregnant woman, injected into a female rabbit, often (but not always) produced *corpora hemorrhagica*—bulging masses on the rabbit's ovaries. A knowledge pattern had emerged, the first shift on the continuum. Unfortunately, technicians couldn't examine the rabbit's ovaries without killing it, so every rabbit died, even if the woman wasn't pregnant. It was an expensive, complicated, and not-altogether-accurate procedure, but the pattern of information it revealed produced more-certain results. Then medical science advanced further. We learned that a hormone called human chorionic gonadotropin (hCG) caused the ovarian bulges, and researchers developed a blood test to detect its presence.[30] Knowledge shifted again to deliver a rule-based solution to the problem: a certain level of hCG in a woman's blood meant pregnancy.

Thus, as medical knowledge grew, the way we attacked the problem shifted along the problem-solving continuum from unstructured problem solving (crude visual and tactile examinations) to pattern recognition (the rabbit test) to rule-based decision making (blood test). Interestingly, once this knowledge became rule-based, a business model innovation occurred in the medical industry. Blood tests were relatively expensive and required skilled technicians to perform them accurately, so many women were nonconsumers. Then, in 1977, in the wake of the discovery of hCG, Warner-Chilcott introduced e.p.t., the first home pregnancy test, which broke both the access and skills barriers to confirm a pregnancy.[31] By moving a medical diagnostic procedure from the doctor's office to the home, Warner-Chilcott democratized critical information, allowing almost anyone to get it.

Certain archetypal business models lend themselves well to problems that lie at different points on the problem-solving continuum.[32] Unstructured problem solving and early pattern-recognition approaches are best delivered by a business model archetype called *solution shops*.[33] Professional service companies like doctors' offices, law practices, accounting firms, and consultancies, all provide customized solutions to unique problems. Their primary resources are people and knowledge. Since neither the outcome itself nor the time invested to produce one can be clearly predicted, businesses of this type usually bill in units of time for services rendered. They tend to be high-margin, high-overhead, low-resource-velocity operations.

As knowledge progresses to clear pattern recognition and rule-based decision making, *value-adding process businesses* produce high-volume solutions at a lower cost.[34] These businesses

FIGURE 21

Business model archetypes

	Solution shop	Value-adding process business	Facilitated network
Customer value proposition	Experts draw on intuition and problem-solving skills to analyze problems and then recommend solutions	Provide scaled products and services to fulfill more pattern-recognition and rule-based jobs-to-be-done at lower cost	Connect users with similar jobs-to-be-done into a system where they can exchange, share, buy, and sell goods and knowledge with other participants
Profit formula	Fee for service, high margin, high overhead, low resource velocity	Fee for outcome, lower margins, low overhead, high resource velocity, scale	Membership subscription, advertising, and transaction-based fees
Key resources and processes	People and knowledge	Predictable processes, integrated systems, manufacturing	Size and composition of customer base; IT system that enables connectivity
Examples	System integrators, law firms, consulting firms, advertising agencies	Retail, manufacturing, education, food services	Consumer banking, online auctions, internet bulletin boards, telecommunications

are integrated-product companies; their success lies in their ability to invent, manufacture, market, and distribute their goods or services at scale. Given the increased predictability, such firms can make their money on actual output (the product or service rendered). These businesses tend to have lower margins and lower overhead than do solution shops; they also have higher resource velocity and depend more on size and achieving target profitability through scale. Their ability to scale is what allows them to democratize knowledge and, ultimately, provide greater access to products and services. Most manufacturing operations fall into this category, and so do such services as MinuteClinic, the pharmacy-based medical kiosks mentioned above.

MinuteClinic recognized that although medical knowledge had changed dramatically since the middle of the twentieth century, the model by which medical care is provided had not. Doctors practice in solution shops—service businesses where difficult problems such as diagnosing Parkinson's disease are addressed alongside simple, well-understood procedures like detecting strep throat. The doctors bring their high-level training with its associated expense to every diagnostic procedure, whether it requires those skills or not. MinuteClinic recognized that advances in medical knowledge had pushed ever-larger amounts of basic medical treatment down the problem-solving continuum into the realms of clear pattern recognition and rule-based care, where less well-trained, and therefore less expensive, nurse practitioners could adequately perform the work.

MinuteClinic took advantage of a shift in the basis of medical knowledge to disaggregate simple rule-based diagnostic procedures from complex, unstructured ones. The innovative business model it wrapped around this CVP broke barriers to consumption of basic medical care. Since 2000, MinuteClinic's decentralized, pharmacy-based kiosks have allowed people to walk in without an appointment and be treated by a nurse practitioner capable of diagnosing a limited number of common low-level ailments using rule-based diagnostics.[35] While this new approach is still scaling (as of 2017, there are eleven hundred locations in thirty-three states and the District of Columbia[36])—and is vulnerable to the ongoing tumult in the health-care sector—MinuteClinic's model represents a legitimate attempt to democratize basic health care by introducing a value-adding process business into an industry long dominated by solution shops.

A third business model archetype, *facilitated networks*, provides the backbone systems by which like-minded customers can exchange goods and services, share information, collaborate, or socialize with little intermediation. Two long-standing examples of this archetype are telecommunications networks and financial exchanges like the New York Stock Exchange. Many more of these kinds of businesses have emerged with the advent of the internet, which, through its capacity to connect individuals to vast amounts of information and to each other, further democratizes knowledge. Online brokerage businesses like eBay, Craigslist, and many of the innovative Web 2.0 businesses, such as Facebook, Twitter, Yelp, LinkedIn, Etsy, Airbnb, and Pinterest, are based on this model, which usually makes money through transaction fees, advertising, or subscriptions that trade on levels of participation in the network.

Facilitated networks democratize knowledge not only by making it more accessible but also by connecting individuals who have incomplete but complementary knowledge. Together, they can dramatically enhance the problem-solving process, shifting knowledge to pattern recognition and rule-based decision making more quickly and more cost-effectively. Think of the open-source movement, where software developers collaborate to improve the Linux computer operating system. Think, too, of the many medical websites that share information about various chronic diseases. The Restless Legs Syndrome Foundation's site, for example, which describes itself as a place where patients can "arm themselves with information to educate health care providers about RLS," is explicitly intended to push knowledge about the condition along through a grassroots effort.[37]

Every day, advances in technology and knowledge, combined with increased access to more information, create opportunities to reach nonconsumers and open new markets. But as we've seen with the examples in this chapter, to democratize offerings with new CVPs will frequently require specialized resources and processes and a different profit formula. Failure to consider how all the elements of the business model work together can doom new initiatives.

In 1997, for example, SAP and Intel launched Pandesic, a joint venture to bring a simpler, less expensive version of SAP's enterprise resource planning (ERP) software to small and medium-sized enterprises.[38] SAP historically targeted huge corporations, but that market was becoming saturated. The smaller-business space—vast, disorganized, and filled largely with nonconsumers of comprehensive ERP solutions—has always been something like the promised land. But the qualities that make it a tempting market also make it a tough nut to crack. Smaller businesses rarely have the resources to buy customized enterprise solutions, the skills to learn how to use them, or the IT departments to maintain them. They are constrained from consumption by wealth, time, and access barriers. The market needs solutions that can break down these barriers, and Pandesic was an attempt to seize this white space.

Being the offspring of two tech companies, Pandesic saw its challenge as strictly a technical problem, and the result, predictably enough, was a disaster. The venture was led by managers who were deeply familiar with huge, complex global organizations, established markets, and well-defined product lines, but who had utterly no experience in identifying and establishing an initial foothold in a new market with a disruptive product. The offering quickly evolved into a complex, automated end-to-end solution, which was neither easy to learn nor easy to operate. The product was marketed through the same channel partners that sold SAP's large company systems—IT implementation consultants such as Accenture. That core sales channel, however, had few incentives to sell Pandesic's simpler product, which didn't need implementation support, when it could make much more money on traditional SAP products. Encumbered by the business model that worked so successfully in SAP's core markets but that was utterly unsuited to the new ones that it was seeking to open, Pandesic shut its doors in February 2001 after having burned through more than $100 million.[39]

SAP failed to develop a unique business model to reach its white space. MinuteClinic and Hindustan Unilever, in contrast, realized that to deliver solutions that break barriers to consumption and democratize markets, they needed new business systems. MinuteClinic's opportunity arose when the basis of medical knowledge shifted. Hindustan Unilever seized its opportunity when the jobs-to-be-done of a large group of nonconsumers at the bottom of the pyramid became easier to address, in part because of changes in government policy. New laws and regulations can create tectonic shifts that open up new opportunities, which is the subject of chapter 5.

The White Space Between

Dealing with Industry Discontinuity

Economic progress, in capitalist society, means turmoil.

—Joseph A. Schumpeter

In the early nineteenth century, most people lit their homes with lamps that burned whale oil. In midcentury, supplies of the oil dwindled, causing a steep rise in price. A Canadian physician and geologist named Abraham Gesner developed kerosene, a cleaner-burning alternative made from a plentiful resource—crude oil—laying the foundation for what would become the modern petroleum industry. Whaling, a major world industry, virtually ceased. Then Thomas Edison threw a light switch, and the world changed again. No one wanted foul-smelling, dangerous kerosene lanterns in their homes anymore when they could have clean and convenient electric light. Demand for fossil fuels plummeted.

The advent of the automobile jump-started the fossil-fuel industry again. Plentiful and cheap carbon-based fuels went on to transform the way we live on the planet—how we travel, heat our homes, and build our cities. The oil industry flourished, the chemical industry evolved on its back, and automobile manufacturers emerged as titans of the manufacturing age. Today, the ramifications of climate change threaten the automobile, utilities, oil, and other hydrocarbon-based industries. The world seems to be on the cusp of a new energy paradigm, one with the potential to radically alter any number of industries as businesses struggle to adapt.

Chapters 3 and 4 focused on innovating business models in response to market-driven circumstances. Those shifts tend to emerge from identifiable and predictable trends that alter industry structures and redraw industry lines over time. But less predictable, more revolutionary forces also exist, forces whose roots often lie outside the marketplace. Consider the commercialization of internet technology; Deng Xiaoping's unleashing of the Chinese commercial dragon with his proclamation "To be rich is glorious"; the attacks of 9/11; the financial meltdown in the autumn of 2008; and the Brexit decision in 2017. Circumstances like these can alter the course for everyone in the race. These acute, episodic events can come with little warning (like a tsunami) or with leading indicators (like a cyclone), but they share two characteristics. First, they dramatically change the game, prompting the need for new customer value propositions and new business models for entire industries and, sometimes, whole economies. Second, the ramifications of these events are extraordinarily difficult to predict. But like the shifts already discussed, tectonic industry change—unforeseen shocks to whole industries—opens up uncharted territories between what was and what is to be, in the *white space between*.

Myriad forces can contribute to tectonic industry change, and they can vary radically from one shock to the next. For the purpose of our discussion, I will focus on three that directly create opportunities or imperatives for business model innovation:

- Unpredictable or radical shifts in market demand (sweeping changes that go beyond the sort of predictable evolution of markets I've already described)

- Discontinuous shifts in technology (that is, the development of revolutionary, enabling technologies)

- Dramatic shifts in government policy targeted at the business environment

Each of these forces can bring about sudden changes on its own, but the three often work in concert to produce even more volatile discontinuities, each influencing and amplifying the effects of the others.

When faced with industry discontinuity, many companies falter. Some fail to recognize the complicated external forces propelling the event, or if they do, they're unable to trace the implications correctly or completely. Others hold tightly to their old paradigms and try to adapt them gradually to meet the changed circumstances. Adaptation in the face of dislocation can help a company ride out the storm, but business model innovation can bring about renewal by creating a new platform that is uniquely suited to the radically altered terrain.

TRANSFORMATIVE MARKET SHIFTS

A business must always be sensitive to changing market conditions, of course, but occasionally, market demand will shift unexpectedly and far more fundamentally than can be reasonably predicted, certainly much more abruptly than the evolutionary shifts discussed in the last two chapters.

You might think the defense industry would have a lot of experience with cataclysmic events, and it does. But that experience has not always translated into changes in its business model. During the Cold War, the US military valued large-scale, expensive, and complex weapons systems that could deter an opponent with the threat of wholesale destruction. Consequently, US military procurement evolved to manage large-scale, expensive, and complex projects, and defense contractors logically built complementary business models: solution shops that specialized in relatively high-margin, low-volume offerings. When the Cold War ended, the industry evolved to some degree. Military operations were downsized, but the era of big, bloated project development and procurement continued.

Then came the 9/11 attacks and the subsequent wars in Afghanistan and Iraq. The nature of combat shifted dramatically, and with it, the marketplace of war. Suddenly, the military, the defense procurement system, and the contractors that served it had to change their ways of working. A centralized, command-and-control mindset had to yield to decentralization if military personnel were to get the information and the versatile weaponry they needed.

The combatants' job-to-be-done when faced with a diffuse enemy in the villages and cities of Afghanistan and Iraq was radically different from what it had been in the Cold War. They needed mobile body armor, better-protected vehicles, and ubiquitous two-way communications, as well as troop-level surveillance and reconnaissance devices—not more-advanced battleships or fighter aircraft. Delivering solutions for the new job-to-be-done of equipping a mobile, fast, decentralized military will require the armed forces to adopt a new business model, one capable of developing and procuring good-enough solutions in volume and in a manner more responsive to rapidly changing conditions on the ground. Consequently, the prime contractors and other providers of equipment and technology for the defense industry will need to shift more of their businesses from solution shops to value-adding process firms with new business models capable of quickly and economically producing this equipment en masse. But they must also retain a part of their business as traditional solution shops to continue to equip the armed forces with large-scale weapons systems.

Another tectonic shift in market demand, which has yet to fully play out, began when China and India opened their economies and brought billions of former nonconsumers into the global market. The advent of microlending further fueled this explosive shift in demand, putting capital and disposable income into the hands of aspiring small-business owners and potential rural consumers, creating opportunities to fulfill a host of new jobs-to-be-done.

If these opportunities weren't tempting enough, there are the related long-term effects of the global financial contraction of 2008 to consider as well; although the world economy has been slowly recovering in the decade since this severe economic downturn, consumer demand in Western markets is still depressed. As demand shifts from West to East, Western multinationals looking for growth must enter these developing markets with new insight and creativity and not expect that simply tweaking their current business models will account for local differences. In that regard, they might look at the innovative models that some emerging-market multinationals are using to great effect. China's Goodbaby, for example, has mastered the trick of offering a vast selection of baby carriages, high chairs, playpens, and the like, at the low end by making up for slim profit margins through the high volume that even niche markets in China can command. Some emerging global companies are already applying that and other lessons creatively to Western markets. The Chinese appliance manufacturer Haier, for example, set up a kiosk in New York's Times Square one hot summer's day and sold seven thousand air-conditioners in seven hours.[1] In any event, no global company, wherever it's based, has the luxury of ignoring this tectonic shift.

TECHNOLOGY-DRIVEN SHIFTS

As my colleague Clayton Christensen first recognized, new technologies are not inherently disruptive; it depends on how well they fit within a company's existing model.[2] Newly discovered enabling technologies can in fact sustain and expand existing markets, strengthening industry incumbents and their current models. The internet, for example, made it easier for Charles Schwab to deliver its no-frills, do-it-yourself discount brokerage services to customers who wanted to manage their own investments. It similarly enabled Dell Computer to be even more effective at selling its personal computers directly to consumers. And it enhanced the existing mail-order-pharmacy business model for Medco, allowing it to provide improved services to both its current customers and millions of new ones before it was sold to Express Scripts in 2012.

And, as we saw earlier, technologies can help companies transform existing markets or create new ones. In chapter 3, we saw how the internet enabled Dow Corning's Xiameter's low-touch, low-cost CVP, transforming its existing market by seizing its white space within. And this book started with the story of how hybrid airship technology presented Lockheed Martin with an opportunity to create a new market by going into its white space beyond.

But, of course, technology that is one company's opportunity is often another company's—or an entire industry's—disruption. In the 1960s, for instance, electric-arc furnaces enabled smaller

FIGURE 22

The industries and infrastructures of each technological revolution

Technological revolution	New technologies and new or redefined industries	New or redefined infrastructures
First From 1771 *The Industrial Revolution*	• Mechanized cotton industry • Wrought iron • Machinery	• Canals and waterways • Turnpike roads • Water power
Second From 1829 *Age of steam and railways*	• Steam engines and machinery • Iron and coal mining • Railway construction • Rolling-stock production • Steam power for many industries	• Railways • Universal postal service • Telegraph • Ports, depots, and worldwide sailing ships • City gas
Third From 1875 *Age of steel, electricity, and heavy engineering*	• Cheap steel • Full development of steam engine for steel ships • Heavy chemistry and civil engineering • Electrical equipment industry • Copper and cables • Canned and bottled food • Paper and packaging	• Worldwide shipping in rapid steel steamships • Transcontinental railways • Great bridges and tunnels • Worldwide telegraph • Telephone • Electrical networks
Fourth From 1908 *Age of oil, the automobile, and mass production*	• Mass-produced automobiles • Cheap oil and oil fuels • Petrochemicals • Internal combustion engines • Home electrical appliances • Refrigerated and frozen foods	• Networks of roads, highways, ports, and airports • Networks of oil wells • Universal electricity • Worldwide analog telecommunications
Fifth From 1971 *Age of information and telecom- munications*	• Cheap microelectronics • Computers, software • Telecommunications • Control instruments • Computer-aided biotechnology and new materials	• World digital telecommunications • Internet, email, and other e-services • Electricity networks • High-speed physical transport links
Sixth From 2003 *Age of cleantech and biotech*	• Renewable energy led by solar, wind, and biofuels • Energy efficiency • Energy storage technologies • Electric vehicles • Nano materials • Synthetic biology	• Enhanced electricity transmission capabilities • Decentralization of power generation • Connection of electricity and trans- portation energy infrastructures • Increased availability of water and electricity • Extensive gene data bank links

Source: Carlota Perez, *Technological Revolutions and Financial Capital: The Dynamics of Bubbles and Golden Ages* (Northampton, MA: Edward Elgar Publishing, 2003), 14.

companies to produce steel at significantly lower costs than those incurred at the large integrated mills of the Big Steel companies. Firms like Nucor and Chaparral Steel wrapped innovative business models around this mini-mill technology and began to pick off customers from Big Steel for such low-end products as construction rebar. In a classic example of Christensen's disruptive innovation concept, as mini-mill technology gradually improved, the smaller companies moved upmarket, nearly wiping out Big Steel and transforming the entire industry in the process.[3]

Similarly, although MP3 compression technology was perfected in the late 1990s, it wasn't until Apple wrapped its innovative iPod and iTunes business model around it in 2003 that the bottom dropped out from under the existing music-retailing model. That same technology, variously evolved to MP4 and other digital-compression technologies, would go on to undercut broadcast television's business model as well, and now streaming technology is disrupting the entire media landscape. Enabling technologies such as these can alter a number of industries simultaneously, creating opportunities for companies in the resulting white spaces.

But if the internet is not inherently disruptive, it has created more new business models than perhaps any new technology since the advent of the light bulb. More than 30 percent of the roughly 350 business model innovations that my colleagues and I studied over the first decade of the 2000s were enabled by internet technology.[4] In fact, the very idea of business models gained prominence with the internet boom of the late 1990s. Think of eBay's auction business model, which hinges on facilitated networks; Amazon's online retail business; or Google's creation of the search market, with its advertising-based business model.

Just as certainly, internet-driven business models have brought many old-guard industries to their knees. It's easy to think of examples. There's the *Encyclopedia Britannica*, whose

CVP was dramatically disrupted over two decades ago by the good-enough *Encarta*, and then further undermined by the not-good-enough *Wikipedia*, combined with the almost limitless resources of Google's search engine. Then there's the travel agency industry, disrupted by online competitors like Expedia and Travelocity, aggregators like Kayak and Trivago, and advice sites like TripAdvisor. Perhaps the most talked-about and widespread disruption is the one going on right now in the newspaper industry.

Newspapers' problems can be (and have been) framed in myriad ways, but a couple of points stand out when we look at their plight through the lens of the business model. Practically from the start, newspaper companies saw the internet as a threat and framed it as such. Most failed to see any opportunities for growth within it. They devised no new CVPs, revenue models, or other ways to change their profit formulas. Instead, they merely took the look and feel of the newspaper and put it online, stretching the resources and processes of their existing model even thinner. Newspapers held on to their business model as a value-adding process, pumping out their product in volume to a mass market, even as their readership gravitated toward more-customized offerings.

In the meantime, the internet-based competition of sites like Google News, the Drudge Report, Yahoo!, Huffington Post, and Breitbart News have segmented and democratized news content—and social media like Twitter, Facebook, and Snapchat have allowed users to curate and share content from multiple sources within their own self-created bubbles. Sites like Craigslist and Recycler have endowed the classified ads job with greater reach. And user-based review sites like Yelp and Chowhound have undermined news organizations' former advantages in local food and entertainment expertise. Each of these new companies has used the internet in a facilitated-network model to capture consumers and advertisers' dollars, while making money in fundamentally different ways. Looked at through the business model lens, the problem newspapers need to address is how they too can leverage the internet to serve their customers' needs for greater customization, while using their incumbent content generation and editorial-filtering strengths to address their new, disruptive competitors head-on.

Interestingly enough, Snapchat, which began as a photo-messaging service in 2011, has emerged as a real pioneer in news generation and distribution. Its news division uses human editors, producers, and reporters to assemble user-generated clips into in-depth stories. Writing in the *New York Times*, Farhad Manjoo called these live stories "transformative," "groundbreaking," and "unlike any other news presentation you can find online."[5] Snapchat's "Discover" feature allows it to collaborate with publishers such as the *Wall Street Journal* and *Al Jazeera* to create stories for its platform, and it also pays flat fees to license content from publishers while retaining the ad revenues that it generates for itself. If Snapchat's advertising-based business model proves viable as it continues to scale, then it could turn out to be a harbinger of a fully digital future for journalism. As I write these words today, Facebook's Instagram has adopted a similar model for content generation—and from early indications, it has stolen some of Snapchat's thunder.

SHIFTS IN GOVERNMENT POLICY AND REGULATION

Though the social contracts that bind consumers and markets together within national boundaries often evolve slowly, dramatic or sudden shifts precipitated by acute political or social forces on the world stage do occur, even in relatively stable, developed nations. Shifts in public opinion, consequent realignments in political leadership, the emergence of new national priorities, or sudden changes in the availability or costs of key resources can result in fundamental shifts in the nature of markets, the jobs-to-be-done within those markets, and the business models that will allow companies to thrive in the new environment.

In the United States in 1973, for example, the deregulation of the health-care industry gave rise to health maintenance organizations, preferred-provider organizations, and a wide range of other new intermediary models. Similarly, deregulation of the European airline industry in the 1990s broke the stranglehold of the national carriers and created opportunities for low-cost entrants like EasyJet and Ryanair. These upstarts tailored their business models to compete on price, democratizing air travel. That policy shift, by extension, altered the landscape of tourism and economic development throughout the Continent, as hundreds of thousands of people who once could not afford airfare suddenly started traveling—many of them to those once-out-of-the-way cities served by the new low-fare carriers.

Public investment in a new social priority can also alter the course of private industry. After India's economic liberalization began in 1991, its tightly controlled corporate environment exploded, allowing new entrants to thrive throughout the nation. A later decision to focus government efforts on village-level economic development and microlending cooperatives created the opportunity for Hindustan Unilever to undertake its Shakti Initiative.

Seeking to understand how these powerful external forces change the jobs-to-be-done in the marketplace and create opportunities for new business models can make the overwhelming far more manageable. Instead of hunkering down and waiting out the storm, or freezing your current model like a deer in the headlights, you can transform and renew your company by building business models that take advantage of the shifting environment. In 2007, the Israeli entrepreneur Shai Agassi attempted to do just that in response to the seemingly intractable problem of climate change. The subsequent failure of this ambitious startup turns out to be an instructive cautionary tale on how even the most carefully laid business model plans can go terribly wrong.

BETTER PLACE: WHAT WENT WRONG?

Since solving the clean-energy challenge will necessarily involve large investments in public and private infrastructure and massive upheavals in mature industries, active government involvement and clear policy direction is crucial. But until Shai Agassi came along in 2007 with his Better Place initiative, what had been missing from the conversation was a comprehensive business model innovation that took all three sets of forces into account: technology, policy, and market.

Agassi's approach to the challenge of creating a mass market for electric cars was a radically new business model geared to seizing an entire industry's white space. As it turned out, Better Place was not a success, but its bold approach is worth examining, because of the stark lessons of why it failed so spectacularly. Agassi began by asking a simple but monumental question: How would people get around in a world without oil? One answer was obvious: electric cars, which have been around since almost the dawn of the automobile industry. But what would it take to spark a wholesale transition to them? The search for an answer has always focused on the technology. Back in 2007, the key resource holding automakers back was the battery. The best batteries were heavy and expensive, took several hours to recharge, and offered a range of just one hundred or so miles.

The industry—and Agassi—was stuck on how to solve for range extension. Then a light bulb went off. What if, Agassi thought, he divorced ownership of the car from ownership of the battery? Instead of thinking of the battery as a durable part of the automobile, what if it was considered part of the energy infrastructure? A new CVP began to take shape: Better Place would build infrastructure in advance of an actual electric car market. Charging locations would be linked by GPS to powerful back-end computer networks, so that drivers would know where to park, and when they returned, their cars would be fully charged. To solve the problem of extended range, Better Place would build battery-switching stations that operated much like car washes. Travelers would drive their cars in, the depleted battery would be removed, and a fully charged one installed in less time than it took to fill a gas tank. The batteries could then be recharged at night, when electricity costs are substantially lower.[6]

So far, this model involved only business forces and technological developments. But as radical as those were, Agassi knew his model would also need the backing and the intervention of the government. He realized that Israel could be an ideal foothold market. With the support of then Vice Prime Minister Shimon Peres, Better Place won agreement from the Renault-Nissan alliance to mass-produce electric vehicles and the batteries needed to run them. In light of his vision and early partnerships, Agassi managed to raise nearly $1 billion in venture capital.[7]

Better Place launched in Israel in 2008 and announced a similar effort in Denmark soon after. The rapidity of the second launch raised a red flag for me when I was writing the first edition of this book. It seemed that the company could better manage its risks if it moved from market to market sequentially, so that it could apply what it learned in one place to the next. Launches were also attempted in Australia, China, and Hawaii, and small-scale demonstration projects were undertaken in Japan, San Francisco, and the Netherlands. None of them scaled successfully. After four years, Better Place had only a thousand cars on the road in Israel and four hundred in Denmark. Agassi resigned as CEO in 2012, and the company declared bankruptcy in 2013.[8]

What are the lessons learned? First off, Agassi seemed to assume that battery technology wouldn't change too quickly. But

Better Place's original infrastructure model required a gigantic capital investment. Battery ranges improved steadily while costs kept coming down, so much so that it became far cheaper to install many high-speed charging stations.

Certainly, Agassi was a better conceptual thinker and salesman than collaborator and entrepreneur. His CVP was limited to one kind of vehicle, offering limited appeal. This limitation arose largely from Agassi's inability to get more automotive OEMs to collaborate and provide more potential offerings. The overall business model was seamless in concept, but again, a more careful test-and-learn approach was needed, as we will discuss in chapter 8. After all, as entrepreneur Steve Blank said, a startup is an organization in search of a business model. Betting hundreds of millions of dollars to scale any brand-new business model before its profit formula is proven is a recipe for disaster.

In summary, the company hadn't sufficiently tested and nailed the real customer's job-to-be-done with a compelling-enough developed offering. This is especially essential in the car business. It took fifteen years for Toyota to reach just 1.5 percent of the US market with its hybrid Prius, and that was considered a major hit. Such gradual ramp-ups suggest caution in spending. By contrast, Better Place was burning through $500,000 per day in operating expenses by the time its first car went on sale.

By 2016, eight years after Better Place's launch, fully electric cars were reaching only 1 percent of new-car sales in the United States and had just surpassed that percentage in many European countries. But these vehicles are far more affordable than they were, and they have a much greater range than they did when Better Place was conceived. Tesla's Model 3 can drive about 215 miles on a single charge and has a sticker price of $35,000; the Chevy Bolt costs roughly the same and boasts a range of 238 miles.

Infrastructure remains a challenge, but it is being solved gradually and at a much lower cost than Better Place envisioned.

Innovators would do well to heed this overarching lesson: don't attempt to scale a business model before testing your assumptions in the marketplace, especially one in which both the technology and its costs are changing fast. We will discuss the test-and-learn approach in more detail in chapter 8.

Now, in chapter 6, we will take a close look at perhaps the most powerful technologically driven shift that we have seen since the dawn of the age of industry—digital technology.

Digital Transformation

*Computers and other digital advances are doing
for mental power . . . what the steam engine
and its descendants did for muscle power.*

—Erik Brynjolfsson and Andrew McAfee,
The Second Machine Age

For all that it's changed how we compute, communicate, and conduct business, the internet is just the tip of the technological iceberg. Artificial intelligence, robotics, 3-D printing, drones, and big-data analytics, to name just a few revolutionary technologies, are changing our world in ways that would have beggared the imaginations of a Jules Verne or an H. G. Wells. But as I hope I've made clear by now, while technology is a great enabler of transformative business growth, it cannot create it on its own.

AMAZON: BUILT TO TRANSFORM

Much has been written about Amazon's steep trail of growth (from about $4 billion in revenues in 2002 to $107 billion in 2015). Amazon wouldn't exist without digital technology, but what has driven its success is its willingness to venture into all its white spaces—between, within, and beyond—and explore new business models.[1]

In 2017, Innosight ranked the S&P and Global 500 companies that have generated the most transformative growth. It based the rankings on the percentage of revenue derived from new-growth areas and the impact these areas have had on the companies' annual growth rates, profitability, and stock prices. Among the top ten, Amazon and Netflix tied for number one, followed by, in order, Priceline, Apple, Aetna, Adobe, DaVita, Microsoft, Danone, and ThyssenKrupp. Not surprisingly, five of those companies were technology companies. While ThyssenKrupp is a heavy-equipment manufacturer, many of its new-growth areas involve software and other digital solutions. Most of Priceline's travel-related products depend on the internet as well.[2]

Amazon survived the dot-com bust of 2000 because, unlike so many of its digital peers, it had a viable and innovative business model that was built around a market-changing customer value proposition and a radical profit formula. After Amazon disrupted the staid book industry, it quickly moved into its white space within, expanding its offerings to include all sorts of other consumer goods. But it didn't stop there.

A few years later, Amazon seized its white space beyond when it devised a new value proposition, offering a commission-based brokerage service to buyers and sellers of used books and third-party sellers of other consumer items. By opening its storefront to partners that a less visionary business might have seen as solely competitors, Amazon moved beyond direct sales to a sales-and-service model, aggregating many sellers under one virtual roof and receiving commissions from the other companies' sales. These commissions more than offset the costs of cannibalization.

After Amazon expanded its IT resources in early 2000, it identified another white space beyond, the IT community. Serving this new customer's needs required different processes, different resources, and a different profit formula—in short, yet another new business model. In 2002, after a careful period of incubation, Amazon launched a web services platform that offered low-cost, reliable, and easy-to-use online services for other websites, as well as client-side applications for web developers.[3] It may have seemed risky for a young company that had only reached profitability in that same year to invest its innovation resources in a new business model (selling technology services on a B2B basis) rather than sticking to its retail core, but business model innovation has paid off. Amazon Web Services posted $12.2 billion in revenue in 2016 and continues to grow, accounting for more than half of the company's operating profit.[4]

And Amazon kept going, straight into the white space between. In late 2007, it hired Gregg Zehr, palmOne's former vice president of hardware engineering, and set up Lab126. Its first product, the Kindle ebook reader, was not only foreign to Amazon's DNA but also potentially disruptive to the entire publishing industry, and of course, it required a completely new business model. To launch a high-margin, product-based offering, Amazon had to become an OEM. Then it wrapped its new technology in a seamlessly integrated iTunes-type digital media platform that combined both transaction-based content delivery and a subscription model for periodical content. It worked with content producers in innovative ways and created an open back end that allowed independent publishers to generate new content specifically for the Kindle platform. In its first year, Kindle sold an estimated half million units and earned high customer satisfaction ratings.[5] With one stroke,

FIGURE 23

Amazon.com: Built to transform

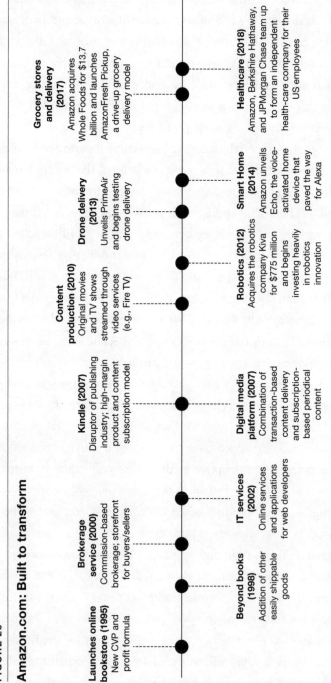

Launches online bookstore (1995)
New CVP and profit formula

Brokerage service (2000)
Commission-based brokerage; storefront for buyers/sellers

Kindle (2007)
Disruptor of publishing industry; high-margin product and content subscription model

Content production (2010)
Original movies and TV shows streamed through video services (e.g., Fire TV)

Drone delivery (2013)
Unveils PrimeAir and begins testing drone delivery

Grocery stores and delivery (2017)
Amazon acquires Whole Foods for $13.7 billion and launches AmazonFresh Pickup, a drive-up grocery delivery model

Beyond books (1998)
Addition of other easily shippable goods

IT services (2002)
Online services and applications for web developers

Digital media platform (2007)
Combination of transaction-based content delivery and subscription-based periodical content

Robotics (2012)
Acquires the robotics company Kiva for $775 million and begins investing heavily in robotics innovation

Smart Home (2014)
Amazon unveils Echo, the voice-activated home device that paved the way for Alexa

Healthcare (2018)
Amazon, Berkshire Hathaway, and JPMorgan Chase team up to form an independent health-care company for their US employees

Amazon had vastly expanded the market for ebooks and made itself a player in newspaper and periodical distribution as well. By 2014, Amazon accounted for more than two-thirds of the ebook market.[6]

From its deepest roots to its greenest twigs, Amazon is built to transform. When it finds opportunities to serve new or existing customers in new ways, it conceives and builds new business models, investing for the future while continuing to extract value from the present. It demonstrates that the process of becoming never ends—and that any organization can change and grow continually, as long as its leaders are willing to invest the time, discipline, and resources in the effort.

In recent years, Amazon has begun producing and streaming original movies and television shows through its video services (which many viewers access via Amazon Fire TV microconsoles, which debuted in 2014). Its voice-controlled smart speakers, the Alexa-enabled Echo family, have put Amazon at the center of not just home entertainment systems, but also smart houses. Whatever its future holds, Amazon's journey is likely to be marked by further transformations as it continues to push out into its white spaces.

HOW DIGITAL TECHNOLOGIES CAPTURE VALUE

While any technology without a viable business model can lead to a commercial dead end, digital technologies *do* drive the formation of certain kinds of business models, creating value in broadly predictable ways. While vastly enlarging our ability to capture, process, store, and transmit data, the business models that they enable fall under four broad categories:

- *E-commerce.* This category includes everything from Warby Parker, which sells designer eyeglasses to online consumers, to Dow Corning's Xiameter, which sells silicone to manufacturers.

- *Digital platforms.* These models allow value-creating interactions between producers and consumers. Think of Airbnb, which connects people who have spare rooms with people who are looking for a place to stay, or Uber or Lyft, which connect car owners with people who are in the market for a ride. Or for that matter, this category can include Salesforce.com, Adobe, and now Microsoft, all of which stream programs and applications to subscribers via the cloud.

- *Models that turn data into assets.* These business models use data management and analysis to derive value from access to, or ownership of, large volumes of proprietary data. Think of Google's targeted advertising; the Weather Company (now a subsidiary of the Data and Analytics business unit of IBM), which delivers 26 billion weather forecasts a day to its subscribers; or GE's Predix, an internet-of-things setup for industrial machinery (see below).

- *Automation-enabled services.* This category of business models harnesses software to do jobs that were formerly carried out by people—everything from the robots that pick and pack in Amazon's warehouses to the autonomous cars that Uber hopes will eventually superannuate its drivers.

Obviously, technology is a double-edged sword. While some platforms enable the creation of new markets and sustainable growth, some simultaneously eliminate potential consumers by substantially devaluing or eliminating their livelihoods.

As businesses explore the new opportunities that technology creates, they must balance their exuberance with appropriate caution. Catchwords like *disruption* and *creative destruction* can be all-too-literally true. Keeping that caveat in mind, let's look briefly at three technology-enabled transformative growth efforts undertaken since the first edition of this book was published—two by established technology players (Microsoft and Netflix), and one from the industrial giant GE.

MICROSOFT BETS ON THE CLOUD

At its annual Build Conference in April 2014, Microsoft announced that it would begin supplying its Windows operating system free to manufacturers of consumer devices with screens smaller than nine inches. The company also made its C# programming language and .NET platform open source, a step that made it easier for developers to create apps that would work across all Microsoft devices. Microsoft hoped these moves would begin to level its playing field with Google, which had always supplied its Android operating system to manufacturers without cost, but these decisions are just the leading edge of a whole new strategy, a huge white space play that has completely changed Microsoft's core business model.

The quintessential high-tech growth story of the 1980s and 1990s, Microsoft hit a wall in the early 2000s, just as the internet was taking off. Then its core business model of selling packaged applications such as Microsoft Office suite was disrupted by cloud-based subscription services, and its business of selling Windows operating systems to OEMs was disrupted by the growing proliferation of non-PC devices, such as smartphones and tablets.

Microsoft's Azure cloud computing platform, a set of subscription services for computing and storage on non-PC devices, was launched in 2010 under the oversight of Satya Nadella, who had been a senior vice president of R&D for Microsoft's Online Services Division. In 2014, Nadella became Microsoft's CEO, a clear sign that the company's new strategy would be "cloud-first, mobile-first." The transition to a subscription model for its software has forced Microsoft to develop new resources and processes around sales, services, and financial reporting and to build and maintain new data centers to deliver its digital services to its customers. Increasingly, the customers for Microsoft's mobile platforms are business users, as opposed to general consumers—a new and different marketplace for Microsoft.

Cloud services now account for a rapidly growing percentage of Microsoft's total revenue, and Azure's leadership in new-growth markets has sent Microsoft's stock on a climb that has outpaced the S&P 500 to reach all-time highs.[7] Acquisitions such as LinkedIn, acquired for $26.2 billion in 2016, will allow Microsoft to place bigger bets on what it believes will be its future: "not technology platforms like operating systems and handsets, but the applications and services that run on top of them."[8] In its 2017 annual report, Microsoft announced that it will be prioritizing AI.[9] Microsoft still has a long way to go before its business model innovations can fully offset its core's decline. But the company's willingness to reevaluate all elements of its business model and push out its white spaces suggests that Microsoft will continue to remain a key competitor in an industry that for almost a full decade (an eternity in the technology business) seemed to be leaving it behind.

GENERAL ELECTRIC'S HIGH-TECHNOLOGY PLAY

For more than a century, GE has been an archetypal heavy-industry manufacturer. But in its 2015 annual report, the company announced its intention to "become a software company, with aims to become a top 10 software company" by 2020.[10] At the heart of this transformation was Predix, a cloud-based operating system that, GE hoped, would allow it to extend itself far out into its white spaces between, within, and beyond. Through this transformation, GE can offer its customers not just the industrial equipment that the company has long designed, manufactured, and maintained but also "complete situational awareness to monitor, and continually improve equipment performance. In practice, it will assure everyone in a given enterprise—whether it's an airline, a hospital, a railroad, an oilfield, or a wind farm—a real-time stream of relevant information, accessible on mobile assets."

The world's first cloud service built for industrial development, Predix is an industrial application of the internet of things. Its platform as a service connects machines, data, and people, allowing the latter to carry out analytics for asset performance management and operations optimization. Machines that GE manufactures itself are sold Predix-ready; devices called *field agents* can be attached to other companies' machines to pull data from them. GE expects Predix to do for factories and plants what Apple's operating system (iOS) did for cell phones.

To launch this transformational business model, GE needed to develop new resources and processes and test new profit formulas. Essentially, it has built a $15 billion software and digital company from the ground up. "Capitalizing on the Industrial Internet may look like just a technological transformation," according to GE, "but it requires real organizational transformation as well."[11] The GE Software Center in San Ramon, California, has more than a thousand software developers and data scientists dedicated to Predix. Additionally, GE's joint ventures, such as Taleris, a collaboration between GE Aviation and Accenture, and partnerships with companies like Intel and Cisco are developing new capabilities that allow GE to deliver quality outcomes to its customers.

An example of such an outcome can be seen in GE's wind farm deal with the global energy giant E.ON. In the past, GE would simply sell more turbines to the company as demand increased. Predix allows E.ON to optimize its current equipment's performance, utilization, and maintenance instead. GE then captures that value by collecting a percentage of E.ON's incremental revenue from its improved performance. Though GE sells less hardware in this new business model, it develops and maintains a long-term relationship that is profitable for both parties.

But as we have seen, transformational initiatives face many obstacles, no matter how ambitious and well funded they are. In June 2017, GE's board removed its CEO Jeffrey Immelt, who had run the company for sixteen years. His successor, John Flannery, has pledged to unload $20 billion of GE businesses while shifting the company's focus from long-term innovation to lifting profits and raising its dividends. Though GE remains publicly committed to Predix, it is clearly hedging its bets.[12]

NETFLIX'S MOVE INTO CONTENT PRODUCTION

Whereas GE is an industrial company that is pushing out into its white spaces by utilizing digital technology, Netflix is moving in the opposite direction. This e-commerce success story is remaking itself with a business model that looks more like an old-style movie studio's.

Netflix began by offering a subscription alternative to Blockbuster's bricks-and-mortar video rental stores—without its competitors' hated late fees. In 2007, Netflix moved into its white space between and began to stream its offerings. Then, in 2011, it made a nearly fatal misstep when it announced that it was splitting itself into two companies, one for streaming and one, Qwikster, for DVD rentals, raising its subscription fees some 60 percent in the process. Eight hundred thousand customers quit, and Netflix's stock cratered, but if the company's fall was spectacular, its comeback was even more so. "In the annals of corporate missteps," James Stewart wrote in the *New York Times* in 2013, "there are few parallels to such a rebound from what once looked like a death spiral, especially in the momentum-driven world of technology."[13]

Netflix's founder and CEO Reed Hastings blamed his company's near-death experience on stupidity and arrogance ("We got desperate and we did some dumb things," he admitted to Stewart) and attributed its recovery to its focus on execution and processes. He said they won "because we improved our everyday service of shipping and delivering. That experience grounded us. Executing better on the core mission is the way to win."[14]

Netflix's next evolutionary phase began in 2013, when it transformed itself into not just a content distributor but also a content creator, releasing the hit series *House of Cards* and *Orange Is the New Black*. Like the original Hollywood moguls, Netflix was laying the groundwork for a new business model with a profit formula that turns on vertical integration—owning its content outright and using its distribution system to deliver that content to its subscribers. As profitable as the iTunes distribution model may be, the content Apple sells to its customers is licensed; Apple must share a significant portion of its revenue with the content owners. So it is with the vast majority of the movies and television shows that Netflix streams or ships on DVDs to its subscribers. But Netflix keeps 100 percent of the revenue it earns from the content it creates itself.

If VCRs and then DVRs (videocassette recorders and digital videorecorders, respectively) helped break the paradigm of "appointment TV," Netflix trained its customers to break the cord altogether and see their television sets (and all their other screens) as searchable libraries that they can use whenever they wish to be entertained, informed, or distracted. Though its self-produced shows account for only a small fraction of what its customers view thus far, they serve the all-important purpose of brand reinforcement. As the video-on-demand marketplace becomes more crowded (Amazon Prime is a major Netflix competitor; as are Hulu and Roku), Netflix's original content reinforces and consolidates its already-towering advantages.

In recent years, Netflix has begun to push into its white space beyond by aggressively expanding its global footprint. The bottom line? With members in over 190 countries, Netflix customers stream as much as 250 million hours of TV shows and movies every day.[15] Between its fall from grace in 2011 and 2016, its annual revenues rose 175 percent, from $3.2 billion to $8.8 billion. At the same time, its base of streaming subscribers grew from 23.5 million worldwide to 93.8 million.[16]

As different as Microsoft, GE, and Netflix may be, each has exhibited the courage to disrupt itself by adapting new digital technologies and putting them at the service of new business models. In this way, these companies have created and captured value in new ways and from new markets.

In chapters 7, 8, and 9, we will turn from the "what" of business model renovation to the "how."

Part Three

Business Model Innovation as a Repeatable Process

*Innovation is risky but it's not random. Innovators have
a disciplined invention process. They may not be able to
articulate it, and sometimes the Eureka! moment happens
in the shower, but it stems from a disciplined process.*

—A. G. Lafley

This book began with a framework to define a business model, one that illuminates the underlying value-creation engine of any business. Part 2 examined various situations that are particularly ripe for business model innovation in existing markets, in creating new markets, and in confronting industrywide upheaval. Part 3 now turns to the "how," shifting from a predominantly descriptive approach to a more prescriptive one.

The companies discussed in the previous chapters have many traits in common. Each had bold and courageous leaders with open minds, an intuitive sense for where transformational growth could be found, and a willingness to reconsider the structure of their existing business models in the pursuit of new customer value propositions. They had imagination, skill, and a bit of luck. What they largely lacked, however, was a systematic approach to business model innovation.

BUSINESS MODEL INNOVATION AS A REPEATABLE PROCESS

From the experiences of the aforementioned companies and those of several other companies I've studied and worked with alongside my colleagues at Innosight and elsewhere, I have extracted patterns and principles and designed a structured approach to business model innovation. Instead of relying on intuition and luck to unlock transformational growth, you can follow a predictable and repeatable process.

This process consists of three basic steps:

1. This step does not involve thinking about business models at all. It starts instead with the opportunity to satisfy a real customer who needs an important job done. The clearer your understanding of the job-to-be-done, the more powerful and enduring the CVP you can develop.

2. You next create a blueprint that lays out how your company aims to fulfill that job at a profit. This is where the business model framework presented in chapter 2 comes in. In conceiving of and comparing this blueprint with your existing model, you will determine if a fundamental business model change is necessary.

3. Then comes implementation—working out in practice how the physical key resources and processes must come together to deliver on the abstract concepts of the CVP and the profit formula. During this step, you'll also decide whether this new business system can be managed in an existing business unit or if you'll need to create a new business unit for the system to flourish.

The job is seldom clearly understood at the outset, and the details of the blueprint won't be completely fleshed out during its initial conception. Managers must consequently understand that business model design and implementation means open-mindedly testing hypotheses and applying lessons learned, not rigid execution.

Chapter 7, then, examines in detail the first two steps in business model innovation, from identifying a job-to-be-done and creating a powerful CVP, to drafting a blueprint of your new business model and comparing it with your existing model. Chapter 8, which focuses on implementation, reveals how to bring your model to life while you maximize your chances of white-space success. Taken together, these two chapters present a fresh approach to developing and scaling a new business—an approach that is useful for startups and incumbents alike. Chapter 9 explores the unique and complex management and behavioral challenges that incumbents face while building new business models or reinventing their existing ones.

Designing a New Business Model

Design is not just what it looks like and feels like. Design is how it works.

—Steve Jobs

Marco Meyrat comes up with a brilliant plan to transform Hilti's tools from a commoditizing product line into a high-end service. Hindustan Unilever creates millions of new hair-care customers by radically reconceiving the nature of distribution. Dow Corning's Don Sheets envisions a new way to capture the low end of the silicone market. As inspiring as these stories are, they can be downright depressing. No one wants to have to depend on something as fickle as inspiration to create a new business.

No one should have to. Conceiving of a truly innovative new business model does not need to be purely (or even mostly) a matter of imagination, inspiration, or serendipity. It can be the result

FIGURE 24

The four-box business model

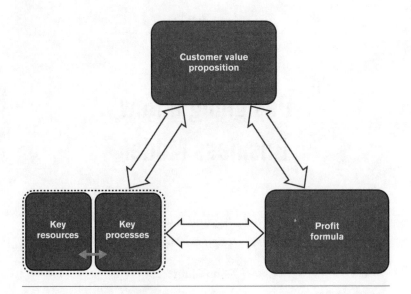

of an orderly process that, like Stanislavsky's acting exercise, uses structure to unlock creativity, rather than the other way around.

The four-box business model that I described in chapter 2 not only defines the parts of an existing business model but also can be used as a framework for building a new one—one that can be used for generating the right questions and assumptions; for organizing and categorizing them constructively; and for implementing, testing, and learning about them in the right order.

As we walk through jobs, CVPs, profit formulas, and key resources and processes in detail in this chapter and chapter 8, keep in mind that business model innovation is an iterative journey. You may need to move back and forth between the boxes before you come up with the right design that makes all four components work together correctly.

As I have emphasized, you are creating a new business model, not extending your current model or a competitor's, or doing what everybody else in the industry is doing, as comforting as those approaches always are. This is about the pursuit of game-changing new growth opportunities, and that pursuit starts with finding important, unfulfilled jobs. This challenging step requires you to look at your market in a new way.

Nothing is more natural, or more difficult to stop doing, than thinking about your market from the inside out—that is, from the perspective of your own company and your existing products and services. But abandoning the inside-out viewpoint is exactly what you need to do. Remember, we're talking about *unmet* jobs, which by definition are those your company is not filling, perhaps to customers it's not serving. You must give up any conviction you may hold that after successfully delivering your products or services to your existing customers for so long, they have no jobs left unmet. Essentially, you should be thinking not like a corporate executive but like an entrepreneur, as if you had not yet sold anything to anyone.

So let's start at the beginning, with the search for an important job a real customer needs to do. I'm sure lots of people have already admonished you to be customer-centric. But what does that really mean?

DISCOVERING THE CUSTOMER'S JOBS

To examine a customer-centric approach, let's consider a case study.[1] A dental device company I'll call DentCo had carved out a profitable niche with a disruptive technology that broke the skills barrier to consumption. The new technology enabled general-practice dentists to perform a tooth-straightening procedure that once only orthodontic specialists could do. When competitors started offering similar products at much lower prices, DentCo faced a choice: it could engage in a price war that would devalue the entire market, or it could find another way to counter the opposition. DentCo turned to its customers to figure out its next step.

Most companies in DentCo's situation would begin their market analysis by asking the dental practitioner (either directly or through a market study), "What attributes do you seek in a dental product?" This kind of survey, called the *needs-based* or *voice-of-the-customer* approach, seems like a sensible way to be customer-centric but it's really not, for two reasons. First, asking customers what they need from your products tends to elicit predictable answers that relate to your products, such as "less expensive," "less invasive," "easier to use," or "more features." Second, a needs-based approach typically segments the target market according to attributes like product features or demographics, but these attributes don't necessarily align with jobs that customers might need to do. The approach either lumps together individuals who want different jobs-to-be-done or, more rarely, separates groups that actually need the same job done. When DentCo originally defined its market segments demographically as general practitioners and orthodontists, it created such *phantom market segments.*

Not surprisingly, companies like this approach. It's relatively easy to collect data on products and demographic segments, and needs-based questions reinforce what incumbents do best— creating sustaining product innovations (like dental products with more bells and whistles, in DentCo's case). If DentCo set out to meet the so-called needs of those phantom segments, it would continue to push its current products and start a price-and-features war with its competitors.

Needs-based analysis is the wrong approach for conceiving of transformative, growth-generating CVPs. To become truly customer-centric, you must stop asking your customers, "What do you need?" and start asking them, "What are you trying to get done?"[2] This is the question that will set you down the road to a jobs-based approach.

When DentCo asked dentists and orthodontists what they were trying to get done during their workday, the question yielded a very different set of market segments and some real answers. To start, DentCo realized that all its customers wanted to build successful practices. That may sound obvious, but it upends phantom segment thinking. It's an important indication that rather than being rigidly separated by specialty, all dental practitioners have much in common. As DentCo dug deeper, it learned what building a successful practice truly means: offering patients the most current care, managing a successful business, and establishing a reputation. By asking what gets in the way of accomplishing these jobs, DentCo identified the major barrier to consumption of existing solutions: time. New products and procedures that would fulfill the job of building a successful practice require new skills and time to train staff members. And to dentists and orthodontists, time is money, since they are typically paid by the procedure, no matter how long it takes.

Now DentCo possesses a truly constructive understanding of its market. Next, it needs to develop a value proposition that centers on convenience, one that can help dentists and orthodontists deliver the most current level of care to their patients while minimizing the time required to adopt new technologies. Armed with this customer insight, DentCo can avoid a ruinous price war with competitors. Instead of adding more features and functions to its products, DentCo can develop a suite of value-added offerings that satisfies the true job-to-be-done for the large general market of all dental practitioners. These offerings could include a time-saving hotline for obtaining expert clinical support, an online forum for sharing best practices, and a staff-training program, all in customizable product bundles. Employing the four-box framework, DentCo can now begin to determine whether it can deliver these new services and capabilities with its current business model or if it needs to create a new one to capture this opportunity.

Focusing on the job-to-be-done gets at the real root of consumer decision making. In his book *The Innovator's Solution*, Clayton Christensen aptly illustrates the concept with the example of a fast-food company trying to improve sales of its milkshakes.[3] Initially, its marketers did exactly what they shouldn't have done—defined the market in terms of its product (milkshakes) and then segmented it further by profiling the demographic characteristics and personalities of the customers who frequently bought them. The marketers then invited representatives from these phantom segments to a focus group, further intensifying the inside-out orientation by asking the group to evaluate the existing product and—even worse—supplying categories of answers by inquiring whether it should be thicker or more chocolatey or cheaper or chunkier. The participants gave clear answers, and the company made changes accordingly.

After the corresponding improvements failed to increase sales, though, the company brought in a new researcher. He made no assumptions about customer segments and didn't ask anyone for suggestions about improving the current product. Instead, he spent a long day watching people in one of the restaurants to see what they were trying to get done when they "hired" a milkshake. He noted the time of day each milkshake was bought, which other products were bought with it, who was with the customers when they made their purchases, and whether people drank the shakes on the premises or sped off in their cars before downing them.

Seen from the job-to-be-done perspective, it turned out that purchasers hire milkshakes to fulfill two distinct jobs, and the primary user in both cases is the same person—a working father. In the morning, Dad is rushing to get to work and doesn't have time to eat a healthy breakfast before he hits the road for his long daily commute. Instead, he buys a milkshake and drinks it in his car. In the evening, Dad takes the kids out for a fast-food dinner and wants to reward them for good behavior with a milkshake after their meal (as we all know, the official Rule Book of Kids says that the most important thing in the world is a treat at the end of the day).

These two jobs dictate two solutions. In the morning, Dad is using the milkshake to overcome his hunger and, as an experience, to alleviate some of the boredom of his tedious commute. He wants the shake to fill time as well as his belly, so he prefers it to be highly viscous and perhaps to have chunks of fruit to make it and the drive more interesting. In the evening, Dad wants the kids to hurry up, so he prefers a less viscous and fruit-free product that they can slurp up quickly. None of that information could ever be obtained by asking people how they liked the milkshake, no matter how marketers sliced and diced the segments, since the same person needed two different jobs done.

Ideally, maintaining a focus on the jobs that customers need to have done is not something you hire a marketer to do when your sales start flagging. That knowledge should spring from paying close attention, in a more ongoing and systematic way, to the jobs your customers are having trouble fulfilling. Hilti, for example, would never have spotted the opportunity to escape commoditization in the tool market if it had not already been in constant touch with customers through regular surveys, both formal and informal, that asked not only about product performance but also about the jobs the customers were trying to get done on the work site. The company also sends videographers and other observers to the sites to watch how its customers use its products and conduct their daily tasks. Had the company simply asked customers what they wanted or needed, it would probably have gotten various replies like "more reliable tools" or "cheaper tools."

A jobs-based approach applies as much to business-to-business companies and to multi-stakeholder situations as it does to direct consumers. DentCo could, for instance, build an even stronger offering, and eventually a more robust business model, by deeply considering the jobs of the patient, third-party payers, and regulators—all of whom share a common interest in the jobs-to-be-done of the practitioner—and then building an offering that accounts for various jobs.

SATISFYING EMOTIONAL AND SOCIAL JOBS

When searching for unfilled jobs-to-be-done, you must think not only about the functional aspects of a job but also about its social and emotional aspects—which together make up the experience that customers desire in accomplishing the job.[4] Hindustan Unilever, for instance, realized that the Shakti ammas would be more successful if they were able to deliver something more valuable to village life than branded products. So as the initiative went forward, the company found it could help boost their social standing by reinforcing the illness-prevention aspects of personal hygiene. This approach made the women more than salespeople; they became purveyors of important social benefits.

Emotional and social jobs are less tangible than practical jobs and thus harder to pin down, yet they must be considered in the development of a new business model. In fashion, for example, social and emotional jobs dominate customer-purchasing decisions. The job of fashion is to "help me feel good about the way I look." This job has functional aspects ("provide something appropriate to my body type, in colors that match my complexion") but far more significant social and emotional ones ("help me fit in, look current, attract a mate, feel confident and sexy, and impress others"). By focusing on these aspects of his customers' job-to-be-done, Spanish retail magnate Amancio Ortega transformed the business model of his retail chain, Zara, and created what Louis Vuitton fashion director Daniel Piette called "possibly the most innovative and devastating retailer in the world."[5]

Fashions were changing rapidly in the 1980s. A new video from a trendsetter like pop star Madonna or rock band Duran Duran, for instance, could be seen everywhere within days, igniting a fad that might last a summer or a year—no one could predict. At the same time, the fashion industry itself was slowing down. Globalization opened up sources of cheap labor, but it also disaggregated internal functions at the big fashion houses. Design and marketing took place on one continent, and fabric sourcing, manufacturing, and finishing on another. Since each step in the value chain required additional time to coordinate, designers had to finalize their products up to a year in advance of the selling season. So, while customers were demanding faster and fresher fashions, designers were pushing last year's looks. Recognizing this dynamic, Ortega envisioned a new type of company, one that addressed the important social job by creating instant fashions: clothes that could be designed and brought to market as fast as demand arose.[6]

Zara needed to fundamentally redesign its key resources and processes—and integrate them in an entirely different way—to deliver its new CVP. It employed advanced automated systems to tightly integrate its retail, inventory, and design processes. It built a state-of-the-art communications system that turned store managers into trend spotters and linked them to in-house designers. Zara assembled most of its clothes locally and built a just-in-time shipping system capable of delivering goods to every store twice a week. Using the best technology of the day, it built an integrated supply chain that could produce garments virtually on demand and ship only the number of items required. With this efficient and responsive operation, Zara could deliver new fashions to market not fifteen months after they were designed, or even fifteen weeks, but in as little as fifteen days.[7]

Guided by the social and emotional aspects of its customers' job-to-be-done, Zara reshaped virtually every part of its business model, adopting an outside-in approach that better served its market while delivering a level of customization and freshness never before seen in the industry. And it did so largely before the information revolution and the internet made customer centricity so much easier.

THE INTERNET AND CUSTOMER CENTRICITY

Thanks to the internet, companies can connect directly with customers and potential markets to learn highly specific information about them, abrogating the need to rely on phantom segments, trend spotters, or needs-based analysis. More important, customers can connect with companies to demand what they want.

Starting in 2000, Threadless built a unique business model to exploit this new reality, using crowdsourcing technology to sell T-shirts entirely designed by its customers. Threadless accepts design submissions on its website from its community of amateur designers and young trendsetters and lets them vote on the products they want to buy. Using mass-customization technology, it then manufactures popular designs within hours, fulfilling the job of keeping its customers' fashions up to the minute through the efficiency of a just-in-time supply chain.[8]

By giving the customer direct control of the company's product design, Threadless has built a thriving community of consumers who feel an ownership stake in its brand. Producing a predetermined demand keeps costs low and margins above 30 percent. And because community members tell it precisely which shirts to make, Threadless never has a flop; every product eventually sells out. "Threadless completely blurs that line of who is a producer and who is a consumer," Harvard Business School professor Karim Lakhani told *Inc.* magazine. "The customers end up playing a critical role across all its operations: idea generation, marketing, sales forecasting. All that has been distributed."[9]

The Threadless model illustrates the power of the customer in a networked world. Now more than ever, success flows from the outside in, from the market to the company. Incumbents therefore need to think creatively about how they can better discern and satisfy the full range of functional, social, and emotional customer jobs-to-be-done.

DESIGNING THE NEW CUSTOMER VALUE PROPOSITION

Having identified an important job-to-be-done for a customer, you then need to create a blueprint of the business model that will satisfy it. Designing a new model begins, of course, with the CVP—the offering that addresses the job at a prescribed price. As discussed in chapter 2, a comprehensive CVP combines in an offering not only what is sold (a product, a service, or both) but also how it is sold. The CVP thus includes how a product or service is made available (access) and how the customer can pay for it (the payment scheme). And as explained earlier, the more important the job, the better the match between the offering and this job, and (usually) the lower the price of the offering, the greater the overall value generated for the customer.

I recommend that you begin designing your CVP by thinking in the most basic terms. With the job-to-be-done firmly in

FIGURE 25

The customer value proposition formula

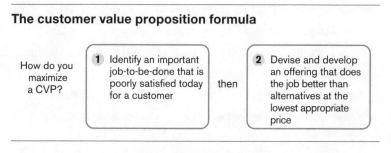

FIGURE 26

Thinking expansively about different CVP components

CVP component	Key questions from the customer's perspective
Offering	• Does the offering satisfy my job-to-be-done? • Does it offer the right trade-offs? • Are the elements that matter the most good enough for what I need?
Access	• How do I get the offering? • From whom do I get the offering? • How often will I need to purchase the offering?
Payment scheme	• What am I paying for? (pay per unit, pay per use, pay when value is added) • When do I pay? (pay up front, subscription, etc.) • What is the form of payment? (cash, credit, finance, exchange)

mind, ask yourself, Can I fulfill it with a product? A service? A combination of the two? In considering the offering as a product, continue to ask questions like, Will it be a durable or a consumable? Will its feature set be limited or extensive? Will it require light or heavy customer support? Will we supply it directly or through distributors? Will customers need to access it frequently or infrequently?[10] Questions about the nature of pricing and payments are similarly basic: Will customers pay in cash or by financing? Will the price be fixed or variable? Will they pay once or in installments?

To visualize these questions, I like to think of each response as a lever that you can push up toward one choice or down toward the other. A final offering can, of course, fall somewhere between the two extremes, but this exercise can be a helpful starting place for thinking broadly about possibilities. The following figures illustrate a range of top-level characteristics that define the basic structure of most CVPs.

As an illustration, consider Dow Corning's model again. Before the company developed the Xiameter low-cost business

FIGURE 27

Sample levers for products and services

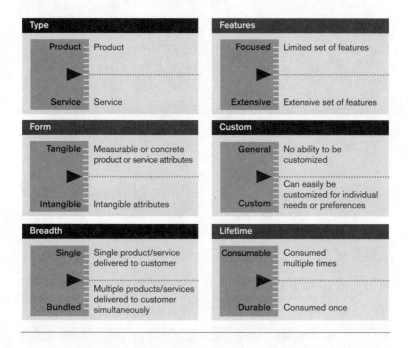

model, Dow Corning's customers bought a combination of silicone products and technical service directly through a highly trained, specialized sales force. They chose from a wide array of silicone product offerings and had an almost unlimited choice of volume options. Ultimately, they purchased a customized offering to suit their unique needs. Xiameter sought to serve a new price-driven customer job with a CVP that flipped the levers to the other side. It limited order sizes and the number of product offerings, which were only accessible online. Lead times, pricing, and payment terms were all fixed as well.

In the case of Hilti, the levers flipped the other way, moving from a commodity product to a high-end service, and from a generalized product to a highly customized one, tailored to the

FIGURE 28

Sample levers for access

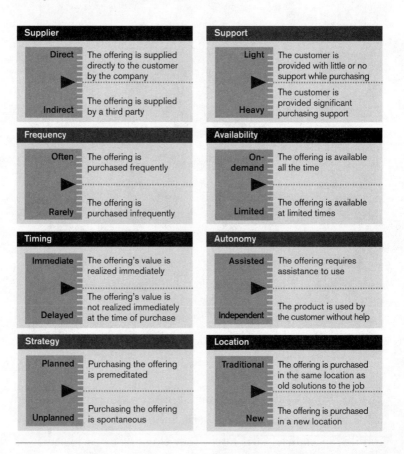

requirements of the individual construction-site customers. Access switched from light support to heavy service and support available practically anytime. The payment system moved from pay-for-product to pay-for-service, with payment now being made in monthly installments.

You can consider dozens of levers when designing your CVP, depending on your particular situation, but to begin, you must focus on those you deem most crucial to the offering. Hindustan Unilever, for instance, zeroed in on the need for much customer

FIGURE 29

Sample levers for payment

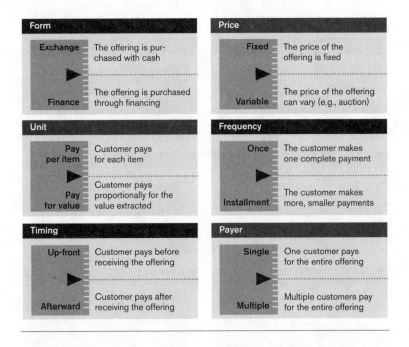

Form		Price	
Exchange	The offering is purchased with cash	**Fixed**	The price of the offering is fixed
Finance	The offering is purchased through financing	**Variable**	The price of the offering can vary (e.g., auction)

Unit		Frequency	
Pay per item	Customer pays for each item	**Once**	The customer makes one complete payment
Pay for value	Customer pays proportionally for the value extracted	**Installment**	The customer makes more, smaller payments

Timing		Payer	
Up-front	Customer pays before receiving the offering	**Single**	One customer pays for the entire offering
Afterward	Customer pays after receiving the offering	**Multiple**	Multiple customers pay for the entire offering

support right from the start, in the form of training and education for the Shakti ammas.

DEVISING THE PROFIT FORMULA

Once you have an idea of your CVP, it's time to devise possible ways your company can make money delivering it. In this regard, I advocate a very different approach from the one most companies use when contemplating new business development.

In traditional business development, executives work in a deliberate, somewhat mechanistic way. They assess the facts and assumptions about the future business environment and then project a growth plan that falls within the core enterprise's usual way of making money. When they come up with a new business

FIGURE 30

Contrasting levers for Dow Corning and Xiameter offerings

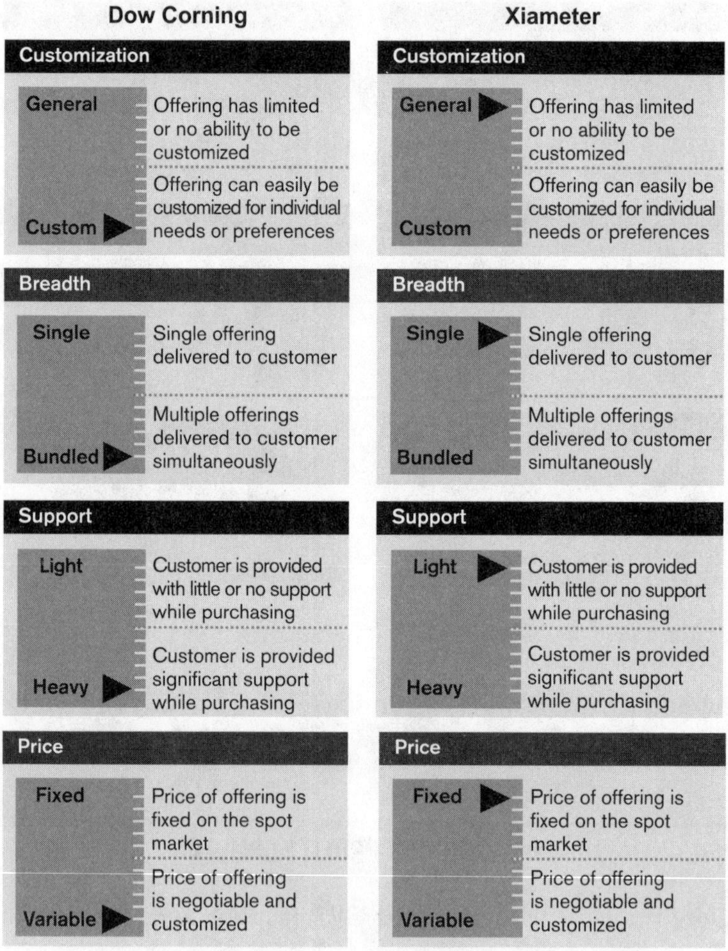

idea that seems to support this plan and conform to the existing financial model, it gets serious consideration and perhaps a green light. But if the idea calls for a different way of making money, the finance people often put on their green visors, sharpen their pencils, and try to graft the established profit formula onto the developing new venture. If the new CVP can't conform to the established overhead structure, margins, rate of return, and so on, it often is killed, a phenomenon I'll revisit in greater detail in chapters 8 and 9.

In designing a business model, you are far better off taking a flexible approach that keeps the focus squarely on the job and on value creation for the customer, not on the profit formula. To meet that end, I suggest working up a range of appropriate financial projections that represent various ways that value could be delivered to the company. The goal is to establish a set of reasonable assumptions that can be tested and modified during implementation in an iterative fashion.

The best you can do at this stage is develop reasonable assumptions about deploying various combinations of resources (people, technology, facilities, and so on) using different unit-margin assumptions about the CVP. Although you will develop different volume or quantity assumptions, you cannot absolutely confirm them in a market that doesn't yet exist. So the right financial approach hinges on assumptions that can only be tested during implementation. In other words, at this point, you should be taking a much looser approach to making money.

"A loose approach to making money?" you might be thinking. "You must be from another planet."

But take a moment to consider this approach. First, the blueprints you design at this stage will most likely be wrong or, more precisely, will probably evolve substantially before you get the formula right. But business being business, it tends to be numbers driven. So, when executives see numbers that look good, they want to lock them in and then do whatever it takes to achieve them. This approach can lead to all sorts of deviations from the goal of fulfilling customer jobs. Offerings will be redesigned, superfluous features added, and essential ones eliminated; resources will be allocated according to short-term financial objectives rather than according to how they serve the CVP. If you finalize a profit formula too early or, worse, are compelled to conform financials to the core business's profit formula, then when things change—as they inevitably will—you'll end up making wrong-headed compromises. Moreover, although you need to arrive at a focused CVP during the blueprinting process, the financials to support it—How much will it cost to make? What is our unit margin or the volume we need to cover our overhead costs? What kind of profit do we need to commit to it?—typically involve a great many assumptions. As your understanding of the new business develops, the choices contingent on the greatest number of assumptions will tend to change the most. Executives who don't understand this are often too quick to kill new initiatives that don't hit their projected numbers right away.

The fact is, implementing a new business model is mostly about managing assumptions. To manage assumptions, you must define them clearly, then test them during the implementation process. That will give you the evidence you need to confirm or reject those assumptions and adjust accordingly. If you develop several potential avenues of profitability while considering profit formulas, you will be better able to adapt to the needs of the CVP without derailing or compromising the offering. This iterative testing of multiple assumptions is what I mean when I advocate for a loose approach to making money. Having a range of choices that you can pursue intelligently as the new model evolves will help you converge on the ultimate profit formula and resist falling back into old habits.

To work up that range of choices, begin by brainstorming as many financial scenarios as possible. One way to help jump-start your creative juices is to think by analogy—to consider how the model for an existing business in another industry might be applied to your context. Not every game-changing business model must be cut from whole cloth; sometimes it's enough to employ a familiar one in a new way. Apple's iPod/iTunes model and

FIGURE 31

Business model analogies

Type	Example	Description
Affinity club	MBNA	Partner with membership associations and other affinity groups to offer a product exclusively to its members, exchanging royalties for access to a larger customer base.
Automation-enabled services	Betterment, IBM Watson	Harness software that automates processes previously requiring human labor and cognition to reduce operating costs.
Brokerage	Century 21, Orbitz	Bring together and facilitate transactions between buyers and sellers, charging a fee for each successful transaction.
Bundling	Fast-food value meals, iPod/iTunes	Make purchasing simple and more complete by packaging related products together.
Crowdsourcing	Wikipedia, YouTube	Outsource tasks to a broad group that contributes content for free in exchange for access to other users' content.
Data-into-assets	Waze, Facebook	Use data management and analysis processes to capture value from having access to or ownership of data.
Digital platforms	OpenTable, Airbnb, Uber	Enable value-creating interactions between external producers and consumers through open, participative infrastructure with set governance conditions.
Disintermediation	Dell, WebMD	Deliver directly to the customer a product or service that has traditionally gone through an intermediary.
Fractionalization	Time-sharing condos, NetJets	Allow users to own part of a product or service but enjoy many of the benefits of full ownership at a fraction of the price.

(continued)

FIGURE 31 (Continued)

Business model analogies

Type	Example	Description
Freemium	Spotify, LinkedIn, Dropbox	Offer basic services for free but charge for upgraded or premium services.
Leasing	Luxury cars, Xerox, MachineryLink	Make high-margin, high-cost products affordable by having the customer rent rather than buy them.
Low-touch	Southwest, Walmart, Xiameter	Offer low-price, low-service version of a traditionally high-end offering.
Negative operating cycle	Amazon	Generate high profits by maintaining low inventory and having the customer pay up front for a product or service to be delivered in the future.
Pay-as-you-go	Amazon Web Services, car2go	Charge the customer for metered services based on actual usage rates.
Razors/blades	Gillette, personal printers	Offer the higher-margin "razors" for low or no cost to make profits by selling high-volume, low-margin "blades."
Reverse razors/blades	iPod/iTunes, Amazon Kindle	Offer the low-margin "blades" at no or low cost to encourage sales of the higher-margin "razors."
Product-to-service	IBM, Hilti, Zipcar	Rather than sell the products outright, sell the service the product performs.
Standardization	MinuteClinic	Provide lower-cost standardized solution to problems that once could be addressed through high-cost customized products or services.
Subscription club	Netflix, Five Four Club, Dollar Shave Club	Charge the customer a subscription fee to gain access to a product or service.
User communities	Angie's List	Grant members access to a network, generating revenue through membership fees and advertisements.

Amazon's Kindle ebook, for example, apply the reverse of King Gillette's blades-and-razor model to digital media.

To fully develop a viable profit formula, you naturally must build an actual profit-and-loss statement. One very useful tool for working up the projections for a business with a new profit formula is a reverse income statement.[11] Rather than starting with revenue, as you would with a traditional income statement, and arriving at profits by figuring costs and then margins, you create a reverse income statement by starting with a profit goal that answers the question "How big does the aggregate profit need to be in three to five years for this opportunity to be worthwhile?" Then you work backward toward defining a viable revenue model, cost structure, and unit margin, using the elements of the profit formula described in chapter 2:

- Revenue model (price × quantity)

- Cost structure (direct costs and overhead)

- Target unit margin

- Resource velocity (inventory turns, staff utilization in professional services firms, etc.)

Revenues are figured by estimating the total quantity of the offering that will be sold and then multiplying that by the price required by the CVP. When you combine that estimate of total quantity sold with the cost of the direct materials and labor required per unit, you can determine the associated allocated overhead cost and then confirm the unit margin needed to reach your profit targets. The resulting profit-and-loss statement represents a set of assumptions about margins, cost structure (including cost of goods sold and marketing and advertising budgets), resource velocity, and the like. In this way, the profit-and-loss sheet becomes a planning document that helps you build a set of testable assumptions.

Ultimately, with a newly formed CVP and a basic profit formula, you are trying to answer two simple questions: Can you tell a story that explains how delivering the new CVP will create strong growth? If so, can you articulate a range of financial scenarios about how you might achieve that success? Each of these scenarios needs to be what musicians call *pure tones*. In other words, the options you develop must be unambiguously differentiated from each other, so that you can clearly analyze their pros and cons.

IDENTIFYING THE KEY RESOURCES AND KEY PROCESSES

In working out a reverse income statement and profit formula, you will naturally begin to identify the key resources and processes needed to deliver the CVP. You will also begin to make assumptions about their cost, availability, and feasibility. Zara knew that to deliver its clothing to widely dispersed retail locations twice a week and remain competitive, it would have to cut costs elsewhere in the business model. It understood that a key process would be its centralized manufacturing-to-shipping value chain.[12] Dow Corning quickly realized that IT infrastructure would be a critical resource for Xiameter and so put IT development at the top of the new venture effort. And for Hilti, backroom contract management was essential.

But while you will be able to identify some key resources and processes during this early design phase, they will become more important in the implementation phase that follows. That's when you will test them to see if you have selected correctly, if you can tightly integrate them with the other elements of the business model, and if your processes will really work.

Before moving on to the implementation phase of a new business initiative, you should stop and compare its blueprint with the business model of your core enterprise. Identifying points of compatibility and differentiation will help guide the next stage in three critical ways. First, by knowing which of the key resources can be taken from (or must be shared with) the core, you can develop a strategy that will allow you to pull them in when you need them. Second, you will be able to identify early on the potential points of conflict where the expectations and habits of the core could interfere with the new effort's success. This will help you understand just how much business model change will be required.

The third and most difficult step is deciding on the disposition of the core. Will the new business model supplement it or ultimately replace it? If the latter, then how much life is left in the core? Enhanced efficiencies can keep it profitable for a long time. DVD rentals account for just a fraction of what Netflix now earns from streamed content—but its decision to segregate DVD sales in a separate company was a nearly fatal error. Apple didn't abandon its computer business, even as the iPod, the iPhone, and the iPad became its biggest drivers.

Managing these tensions requires mastery of the art of what I and my colleagues Scott Anthony and Clark Gilbert have called *dual transformation*.[13] As CEO of Salt Lake City's *Deseret News*, Gilbert created a two-track process to help the company adapt to its digitally disrupted marketplace, downsizing and otherwise streamlining the original print paper, positioning on a new job-to-be-done with a shift from a local to a national audience, and building a separate portfolio of digital products that was positioned for growth. But as we will see in chapters 8 and 9, core businesses rarely fade quietly, even when the writing is clearly on the wall. For this reason, core businesses pose the greatest threats to new initiatives.

8

Implementing the Model

The characteristic of scientific progress is
our knowing that we did not know.

—Gaston Bachelard

A **great business model blueprint** is a powerful first step toward
seizing your white space. But a theoretical blueprint can't be
turned into a working business in one leap. A working business
must be the culmination of a process of controlled experimentation that proceeds in small steps. Hypotheses are put forward
and tested, and the lessons learned are used to make necessary
adjustments as you go forward. In this way, you will discover if
the new model won't work in practice or how it needs to change
so that it will work before you put very much at risk.

This is how I use the term *implementation*: an effort largely
focused on testing and validating assumptions while integrating
the key resources and processes required to deliver on the CVP
and the profit formula. Implementation should be pursued in

FIGURE 32

Stages of business model implementation

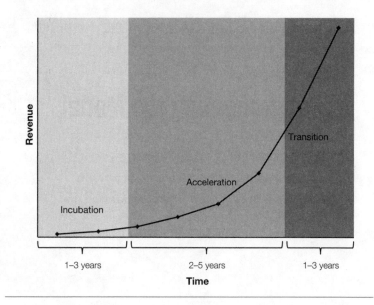

three stages: incubation, acceleration, and transition.[1] Incubation should be focused on establishing profitability, but it's critical not to put pressure on the project to reap revenues at any great pace until the acceleration begins. Real, large-scale revenues seldom accrue until the transition stage.

INCUBATION

Incubation is the process of identifying the assumptions most critical to the success of the business proposition and then systematically testing them in a targeted manner to quickly prove or disprove their viability and, by extension, the viability of the new initiative. You must have creative problem-solving and a discovery-driven approach to project planning at this stage.[2]

The immediate goal isn't necessarily business success; it is new learning. Business leaders should demand clear answers, even if those answers come from failures.

"For every one of our failures, we had spreadsheets that looked awesome," jokes Scott Cook, the founder of accounting software pioneer Intuit.[3] As the leader of a highly innovative company, Cook learned the value of focused testing through experience. A team once brought him a proposal for a business that paired accountants who had available time on their hands with those who had more work than they could handle, essentially transforming a local service market into an internationally networked one. Accountants, the team assumed, were very good at counting but not as skilled at marketing or acquiring new clients. The team had gone quite deep in its analysis, producing detailed spreadsheets based on all sorts of noncritical assumptions about the idea's potential profitability. It seemed to be a brilliant idea, but the team had no hard data.

"Instead of working nine months to build the whole service," Cook says, "I asked, 'Can you find a way to test quickly the supply hypothesis?' So the team hacked together something in three weeks—had humans doing stuff behind the scenes instead of the computer—and sent a little test mailing to fifty thousand accountants. By the fifth week they had proved—at virtually no cost—that there were good accountants sitting unused."[4] And they kept learning. The team continued to develop the project, launching one piece every few weeks, following this test-and-learn approach.

Typically, new business initiatives fail because the people responsible for them take assumptions to be fact. They don't work hard enough or systematically enough to identify and validate critical assumptions before either committing large resources to the business proposition or walking away. Managers need to test early, test cheaply, and test often. Investing a little to learn a lot helps overcome the uncertainty of new business development.

"Fast testing is risk reducing," concludes Cook, "and most people are happy pursuing risk-reducing behavior. Once the value of this approach becomes apparent to all, it becomes part of your innovation culture. New teams, rather than commit large resources to vague planning, begin to ask early on how they can test their key hypotheses."[5]

To successfully incubate a new business, you must identify a *foothold market*, a small geographic region or customer group that will serve as the low-cost laboratory. Preferably familiar or otherwise friendly, the foothold market nevertheless needs to represent the larger target market you intend ultimately to pursue.[6] Hindustan Unilever tested the Shakti Initiative in Andhra Pradesh, a state in southern India, and started with just seventeen women, slowly expanding the number as the company learned what it needed to succeed. Hilti worked out the resources and processes of its white-space play with a few large clients in its base market of Switzerland before slowly rolling out its model worldwide. Incubating a new business in your white space is filled with uncertainty, but it needn't be filled with risk. Foothold markets allow for safe, low-cost, structured testing that yields demonstrable results.

Most critically—and I cannot stress this enough—you must keep the incubation effort free of interference from the core and the way it operates. "Part of the creative challenge is not having too many controls," says Netflix founder and CEO Reed Hastings. "We manage new innovation through context, through values and influence, rather than control. We talk about supporting innovation, rather than managing, controlling, or proceduralizing it, because it's so creative."[7] This is another way of saying that incubation should be oriented toward deploying key resources rather than refining processes.

A Tale of Two Low-Cost Carriers

While incubating a new business model, pay attention to the relationships between all its key elements, and monitor how well the sum of all the elements supports the CVP. Models whose elements don't mesh well almost always fail.

Consider the stories of Southwest Airlines and Delta's Song Airlines, two low-cost airlines that achieved vastly different results. Southwest Airlines is generally credited with starting the low-cost airline revolution; its story has been told many times. Song was a dismal failure whose story has been forgotten. But viewing both ventures through the lens of the four-box business model shows how important internal consistency was to Southwest's success—and how a lack of it contributed to Song's demise.

At its inception, Southwest targeted regional commuter customers whose needs were being ignored by the big carriers. These customers were mainly Texas residents who couldn't afford air travel and were taking the bus between cities like Austin and Dallas. They were nonconsumers, and Southwest astutely realized that if it was to capture them, it would be competing not against other airlines but against bus travel. The airline set out to satisfy the commuters' job-to-be-done by providing faster transportation at a price nearly comparable to a bus ticket. This CVP put necessary constraints on Southwest's profit formula. To deliver revolutionary low prices, the airline would have to keep margins low, and to make money at those margins, it would need to keep direct costs and overhead low and resource velocity high. It would have to find ways to get more turns from its capital equipment.

As the company began to develop the key elements of its model, it made choices to support these requirements. For instance, Southwest adopted a direct-sales model for tickets, eliminating travel agent fees. Removing this intermediary also put payments in the company's hands more quickly. Customer service could be high touch (friendly behavior is cheap), but expensive extras like food and entertainment were trimmed or eliminated. On the resource front, the airline chose to use a single type of plane to streamline repair and maintenance costs and relied heavily on electronic systems to run sales channels. Externally, Southwest chose to fly into secondary airports, whose lower gate fees reduced operating costs. It also negotiated industry-rule-breaking profit-sharing contracts with its pilots' union, thus trimming another traditional source of high costs.[8] Finally, it entered into long-term contracts for fuel.

These key resources all supported both the CVP and the profit formula. Secondary airports and standardized maintenance procedures—aided by a point-to-point routing system that decreased the waiting times associated with industry-dominant hub-and-spoke routing—produced industry-leading turnaround times, maximizing asset velocity by keeping planes flying a greater percentage of the time.[9] And Southwest's decision to do away with reserved seating and to institute a first-come, first-served approach got passengers on and off planes faster. Taken together, these choices formed a cohesive model that reinforced Southwest's CVP and led to great success.

Years later, legacy carrier Delta attempted to enter the low-cost travel business. It launched Song, aimed at "discount divas," female leisure flyers who wanted the convenience and affordability of a low-cost carrier coupled with a sense of style. In addition to serving a more refined customer segment, Song's CVP differentiator was a "hip" approach to travel. It was a white-space-within play for Delta, but the company failed to recognize it as such. Like Southwest, Song's profit formula relied on low margins, low-cost drivers, and high resource velocity, a strategy that might have worked but for the incongruity of the other elements in its model.

FIGURE 33

Success of Southwest Airlines

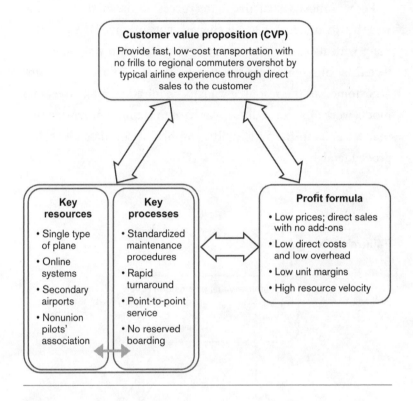

Customer value proposition (CVP)

Provide fast, low-cost transportation with no frills to regional commuters overshot by typical airline experience through direct sales to the customer

Key resources	Key processes	Profit formula
• Single type of plane • Online systems • Secondary airports • Nonunion pilots' association	• Standardized maintenance procedures • Rapid turnaround • Point-to-point service • No reserved boarding	• Low prices; direct sales with no add-ons • Low direct costs and low overhead • Low unit margins • High resource velocity

Emulating Southwest, Delta chose a single type of aircraft flying point-to-point routes, which it hoped would produce faster turnaround times and higher resource velocity. But to serve its divas, it retained reserved seating and added lots of frills, like organic food, custom cocktails, personal entertainment systems, designer uniforms for flight attendants, and an in-flight exercise program. All these perks either added costs or slowed turnaround by increasing restocking and cleaning time. Fun, fashionable service is not fast, efficient service. These conflicts in the model were difficult to reconcile. Flying to primary airports further increased costs and impeded resource velocity, as Song jets struggled to move quickly on crowded runways amid busy infrastructures.

Perhaps most destructive to the success of the model, however, was that in an effort to avoid alienating its unions, Delta saddled Song with its existing pilots, crews, and machinists. Long protected by high-cost union contracts, these employees were unaccustomed to the resource velocity required to make the Song model work. The core culture was hard to change and caused further tensions in the system. These inherent conflicts ultimately proved fatal.

FIGURE 34

Failure of Song Airlines

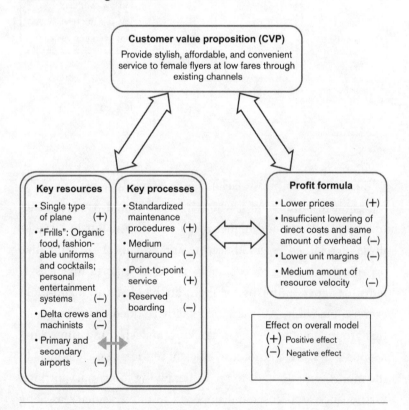

Southwest's and Song's business models both had strong CVPs serving specific jobs-to-be-done, and both featured differentiators designed to serve those jobs (you might question the discount-divas concept, but at least it was clearly defined in Delta executives' minds). But Southwest perfected its model in small foothold markets before gradually expanding to national service, whereas Delta bet the bank on a business model whose elements, it turned out, couldn't mesh and therefore could not support Song's CVP.

Profit before Revenue Growth

Early in the incubation process, the business model framework helps identify the new value propositions that have the greatest chances of success and weed out those that contain fatal flaws or inconsistencies. You must also clearly define what will constitute success and how you will measure it. Some of the best-conceived initiatives have gone down in flames from such common errors as an overeager push for scale, overinvestment in imperfect or untested assumptions, and a lack of patience with a process that needs more time to gel.

Transformational business models should demonstrate the success of their fundamentals quickly by delivering value to the customer and profits to the company. Hindustan Unilever predicted the eventual success of the Shakti Initiative on the basis of early profit accrued from just a few dozen Shakti ammas. Xiameter started filling the production pipeline and clearing profits almost immediately after it refined the stringent business rules needed to serve its commodity market. The evidence of profitability demonstrated early on by Hilti's initial eight customers gave Marco Meyrat and the other company executives confidence in the tool-leasing service. That confidence granted them the patience to scale up in a measured way in their initial foothold market of Switzerland and beyond.

This is one of the great benefits of using the business model framework in new-product development. The earlier and more explicitly you focus on the initial key assumptions that define that framework, the easier it becomes to identify and evaluate the proper metrics for success. Having clear definitions of your CVP, profit formula, and key processes and resources, combined with the right approach to business model blueprinting and implementation, provides you with the structure you need to significantly reduce the investment and execution risks of ventures in your white space. Reduced risk means reduced fear. When your white space is safer, you can explore it more systematically.

Successful incumbents may initially dislike revisiting the uncertainty they have worked so hard to banish. But you must learn to manage the paradox of embracing uncertainty while methodically working to stamp it out. You need to build tolerance for initial failure; sometimes, it can show the way to great success. In 1999, for example, Amazon introduced an eBay-like auction model to engage third-party sellers. The experiment was widely viewed then as an abject failure, but it was an important step toward a strategy that Amazon eventually pursued with great success. "The basic thought was: 'Look, we have this Web site where we sell things, and we want to have vast selection,'" says CEO Jeff Bezos, relating a story he often shares at company events:

> One of the ways to get vast selection is to invite other sellers—third parties—onto our Web site to participate alongside us and make it into a win-win situation. So we did auctions, but we didn't like the results . . . Next we created zShops, which was fixed-price selling, but still parked those third parties in separate parts of the store. If a third-party seller had a used copy of *Harry Potter* to sell, it would have its own detail page, rather than having its availability listed right next to the new copy. We still didn't like the results we

got. It was when we went to the single-detail-page model that our third-party business really took off. Now, if we're offering a certain digital camera and you're a seller with the same camera to sell, you can go right on our own detail page, right next to our product, and underbid us. And if you do, we will put you in the "buy" box, which is on that page.[10]

Clearly defining the metrics of success gives you a clear path toward achieving it, better enabling the nascent initiative to absorb its inevitable early failures. As assumptions are tested, success or failure increases the knowledge in the system. If the enterprise gains traction and turns the corner toward viability, demonstrable knowledge takes over.

ACCELERATION

Once you've proven that a new model is viable through a well-staged incubation effort, it's time to step on the accelerator. The knowledge side of the equation is substantially higher now, so here you focus less on experimentation and more on setting up repeatable processes to make your business profitable. Acceleration begins by refining and standardizing processes, establishing the business rules that govern them, and defining the metrics that chart continuing success. Over time, these rules and metrics are internalized as norms; people think of them as "the way things get done." Imposing such controls maintains quality and customer satisfaction as the business expands. These controls must be monitored and refined as the new business reaches each stage of growth to make sure the various business activities involved are still in harmony with one another.

Shifting from incubation to acceleration means moving from footholds to broad market adoption. Zara became one of the world's fastest-growing and most successful clothing retailers in part because of the patience with which it accelerated its business model. In the first fifteen years of its life, Zara expanded only in Spain, establishing strong profitability in this home foothold market.

It did not open its first international store until 1988, and then only in nearby Oporto, Portugal. The following year, it crossed the pond to the United States but found little success there.[11] The company realized that the challenges of internationally scaling up a model based on centralized manufacturing and control required significant adjustments to both its value chain and profit formula. Specifically, it needed to design a highly advanced communications system that would allow its vertically integrated production model to extend successfully to remote locations. But because Zara's investment in this overseas test was minimal, it was able to bring the key resources to bear and evolve the model to develop the needed capability.

In 1990, Zara entered the French market and found greater success. It quickly began adding new stores in major city centers throughout the country.[12] Each market provided further opportunities to experiment and adjust. "Trial and error is a key part of our model," says a company spokesperson.[13]

Zara's patience for growth and its willingness to explore different ownership paradigms—company-owned superstores on the Continent, franchises in Russia, partnerships elsewhere—helped it understand what its innovative model was ideally suited to do, and just as important, what it was not. Over time, the company streamlined processes and concentrated acceleration efforts where they would be most likely to succeed.

Hindustan Unilever had a similar stop-and-go experience with its Shakti model. It successfully grew the business from twenty-eight hundred to forty-five thousand Shakti ammas in just a couple of years, but as it contemplated the next stage of growth, it identified key processes that needed refinement if they were to support the much larger scale it envisioned.[14] The initiative was held to forty-five thousand representatives for some two years while the model was tweaked to handle the logistical challenges of higher volume and while new educational tools were created to meet the needs of a much larger and diverse audience. By 2015, Hindustan Unilever not only had expanded the Shakti Initiative to seventy thousand Shakti ammas, but was also exporting variations of the Shakti business model to Bangladesh, Vietnam, Egypt, Sri Lanka, and other countries.[15]

Both Zara and Hindustan Unilever expanded intelligently and deliberately while controlling risk. Throughout their acceleration processes, they vigilantly monitored how the elements of their models were holding up and working together, and they changed their rules and metrics and sped up or slowed down as necessary to protect and perfect their new businesses.

TRANSITION

The final stage of implementation applies only to incumbent enterprises. It addresses whether the new business must be reintegrated into the core or remain a separate unit to thrive.

I believe that the highest likelihood of success accrues to efforts that are kept fully separate from the core, from the beginning of strategy development until well into the life of the new business. Most companies operate in a culture of advocacy: units or silos protect their turf and push for what they want and need. Such infighting can crush attempts at business model innovation. "A large segment will always dominate a small one," says Terry Kelly, president and CEO of outdoor apparel at the plastics technology company W. L. Gore & Associates. "You must think carefully about dividing and segmenting so that emerging opportunities are not stifled. Leaders must determine how to divide in order to multiply."[16]

Determining the ultimate disposition of a newly developed business model should, of course, be guided by management's judgments about the operating conditions that will give it the greatest chances of long-term success. But all too often, a model's unique characteristics are overlooked because of a knee-jerk desire to consolidate operations. As a general guideline, a new business model should probably be kept separate from an existing business unit when any of these conditions apply:

- It calls for a significantly different set of business rules and accompanying metrics, which will evolve into significantly different norms.

- It requires a distinct brand with a promise very different from that of the core brand to fulfill its CVP.

- It tends to be disruptive to the core business model (that is, it makes money with a much lower margin) and requires a much lower overhead structure, a much higher resource velocity, or both.

On the other hand, it may be possible to reintegrate a new business into the core under any of the following circumstances:

- It differentiates itself mainly in its resources and processes, but its profit formula is substantially similar to the core's or provides greater unit margins.

- It enhances the core brand in some significant fashion.

- It can transform and improve the core business model.

As we saw in chapter 3, Xiameter discovered that it needed autonomy from Dow Corning's core operations very early in its incubation process when Don Sheets set up his experimental war game to gauge how existing staff and systems would react to the requirements of the new CVP. "The results were not positive,"

Sheets says, "but it was the best thing that could have happened. If we had gotten caught up renegotiating and attempting to agree on everything with regard to the Xiameter brand, we'd still be waiting to launch it. Many efforts, when they lose a war game like that, are folded or significantly redirected. It just made it clear to me how we needed to be separate."[17]

Hindustan Unilever paved the way for the possible integration of Shakti by accruing all early profits to the core and having Shakti employees work side by side with their Hindustan Unilever colleagues. Once Shakti had grown to sufficient scale to prove its worth and not get smothered, company executives determined that the unit would benefit from the added resources of the core. Though there were clashes of organizational culture during the transition, the model has so far been successful because the ground was well prepared and the company culture valued entrepreneurial achievement.

Hilti devoted little serious consideration to whether the new business model could be nurtured and operated successfully within the core or would need to be a separate unit. But since the new model called for higher margins than the old did, integration made sense. And it didn't hurt that Hilti had a history of successful transformations: its adaptable organizational culture was uniquely suited to change.

For the purposes of explicating the business model innovation, I'm calling transition the last stage, but integration issues must be considered throughout the incubation and acceleration stages. Building a successful new business model requires that incumbents constantly test and evaluate it against their existing business model to see what conflicts arise. For that reason, incumbents have to thoroughly analyze and articulate the key elements of their current business model before embarking on building a new one. This point cannot be overstated. While it should be a given that successful companies understand the model that is driving their success, surprisingly, they often don't. Before you can renovate a business, you must first peel away the veneer of everyday operations and understand the business model at its core—how it works, what it enables, and what it inhibits.

BUYING NEW BUSINESS MODELS

Organic new growth is far from a sure bet. New businesses can take years to mature. The skills needed to conceive and incubate them, as we have seen, present unique challenges that many companies find difficult to overcome. "A large enterprise has trouble making an investment in innovation," says Brad Anderson, the former CEO of electronics retailer Best Buy. "It's in part because Wall Street has trouble imagining a new way to operate but, more important, because people inside the company can't see the value of a new idea and so won't allocate the resources and support the new initiative needs to succeed."[18]

Organic growth is not the only option available to companies seeking transformational growth. Although most of this book has been dedicated to developing new business models within incumbent organizations, incumbents can also achieve transformative growth and exploit opportunities in their white spaces through acquisition. When Anderson took over Best Buy, he led the company through a series of strategic acquisitions that helped it grow beyond a pure retail sales model.

Some companies are legendary for their acquisitive prowess. For a time, GE acquired dozens of companies a year. Cisco has made more than one hundred acquisitions in its thirty-two-year history. Most acquisitions are pursued because they have the resources and capabilities that can be integrated into the buyer's existing business model. Acquisitions can also be a way to quickly spur sales and develop reputations. They can allow mature organizations to brand an emerging company as "most likely to succeed" or steadily pursue sound strategic growth.

But study after study has found that acquisitions typically tend to disappoint; business scholars have variously estimated that half to as many as 80 percent fail to create value.[19] The high-profile struggle of AOL after its $180 billion acquisition of Time Warner is one spectacular example of an acquisition gone bad. But there are others: Quaker Oats paid $1.7 billion for the Snapple brand in 1994 but sold it to Triarc three years later for a mere $300 million.[20] After spending $36 billion to merge with Chrysler, Daimler-Benz sold it to a private equity firm for just $7.4 billion.[21]

By this time, you won't be surprised to learn that I believe that many if not most M&A disappointments stem from a failure to understand the fundamentals of business model development. Companies often acquire other companies without fully understanding what they're buying. New resources or products can be folded into the core, but new business models resist. The success of an acquired model frequently lies in its processes and its profit formula and very often in the wholly interdependent, integrated nature of its model.

Johnson & Johnson well understands the difficulty of quickly absorbing new business models; it buys businesses at early stages of their development and keeps them separate until they can be safely integrated into its core. Its Medical Devices & Diagnostics division (called Medical Devices since 2016), for example, bought three businesses with models that were fundamentally new to its respective markets: Vistakon (disposable contact lenses), Life-Scan (at-home diabetes monitoring), and Cordis (artery stents used in angioplasty procedures). J&J bought them young and slowly incubated them into the larger enterprise, where they were growth engines for many years.

Most of the principles that govern the incubation, acceleration, and transition of homegrown new business models also apply to acquired ones. Equally important is the willingness of leadership to allow a newly acquired business model to pull what it needs from the core, rather than pushing elements of the core model onto it. As Vijay Govindarajan and Chris Trimble noted in *Ten Rules for Strategic Innovators*, a newly acquired business based on a model distinct from the core should decide what it can borrow from the parent, what it should forget, and what completely new practices it must do or learn.[22]

Best Buy's Brad Anderson expressed this idea succinctly when asked about the company's acquisition of Geek Squad, an in-home computer services and support company: "Geek Squad bought Best Buy. Not the other way around."[23] Anderson knew that the synergy would produce growth and transform the company, but he also knew that the low-margin, high-volume retail mentality of Best Buy could easily suffocate the high-touch, high-margin service orientation of Geek Squad. He let Geek Squad pull from Best Buy what it needed to thrive. At the time of acquisition, in 2002, Geek Squad had sixty employees and was booking $3 million in annual revenue. Within three years, Geek Squad's twelve thousand service agents, working out of seven hundred Best Buy locations across North America, clocked nearly $1 billion in services and returned some $280 million to the retailer's bottom line. In 2017, Geek Squad had twenty thousand service agents spread across eleven hundred locations.[24]

Overcoming Incumbent Challenges

*It's the same each time with progress. First they
ignore you, then they say you're mad, then
dangerous, then there's a pause and then you
can't find anyone who disagrees with you.*

—Tony Benn

C onsider a fictional corporation, DogCorp, the world leader in
the manufacture of high-quality dogs. DogCorp makes great
dogs, cutting-edge dogs—the best, most efficient, most innovative dogs in the market. For years, sustaining innovations have
allowed DogCorp to post steady growth and earnings, consistent success that has made it the company of choice for talented
dog designers and managers throughout the industry. As its
pack has grown, DogCorp has built a strong corporate canine
culture.

One day, a fairly new manager realizes that, as much as the market loves the pooches DogCorp makes, a significant number of customers need a different kind of pet, a more independent and curious animal, and that this need is not being served. Excited by this new market growth opportunity, she puts together a team that designs something new—a cat—to satisfy this unmet need. Then she brings it to her superiors.

And the DogCorp managers go rabid. Pack meetings are called. The financial pit bulls have bones to pick. The poodle managers sit around waiting for some other breed to pet the cat, to signal that the intruder is not dangerous. The hound division stalls; no one there will be promoted for championing a cat, so they just sit and growl. As promising as this cat thing seems, something about it doesn't smell right to any of the canine capitalists at DogCorp.

Companies innovate all the time. They innovate products. They innovate marketing efforts. They innovate processes to increase efficiency. Most of these efforts improve their existing business model incrementally, streamlining and increasing its efficiency, tweaking the profit formula, bringing new key resources to the table, and changing and refining individual processes. But rarely do incumbent companies make the leap to reinvent their existing business model or create a new one in response to an opportunity or threat presented by a new customer value proposition. Many well-intentioned companies find their innovation efforts thwarted by unknown forces within their own organizations. Forward-thinking strategies are hammered into old familiar shapes. Initiatives with promising starts are derailed by powerful constituencies protecting the status quo. Earnest efforts unwittingly render mundane the most exciting new idea.

Why does this keep happening? The business model framework suggests a rational answer. If the core business is successful, it should not be surprising that everyone in the organization is loyal to the model underpinning its success. To be fully open to the kind of transformative opportunities that require new models, we must understand how the existing business model works, through all its many parts, to preserve the status quo, just as it was designed to.

WHO LET THE DOGS OUT?

There are many ways to skin a cat, the old cliché goes, and just as many ways to kill one. Typically, DogCorp stops nascent kitten ideas before they ever see the light of day. Its managers screen them out from inception, letting only puppies pass through to the marketplace of new ideas. For those kitten ideas that do make it through, the threat of death by dog is far from over as three other dangers lurk. Most commonly, DogCorp will kill off the potential for any cat development through benign neglect, a phenomenon we can call the *non-dog dilemma*. Managers, being smart, recognize the DNA of projects familiar to the corporation's core. A cat lacks the genetic markers identifying it as canine, so when it starts scratching around for something to sustain it, it is not invited into the kennel. It is non-dog, and that is often reason enough for managers to lock the doors. Fundamentally new CVPs, ideas that require different profit formulas, or projects that call for different key resources and key processes can all look like non-dogs. If managers could recognize them as *cats*, they might find potential uses for them or see untapped markets or underserved consumer needs they satisfy. But instead, all thinking stops at *non-dog*.

Non-dogging manifests itself in companies as a failure to allocate resources, and it can occur up and down the corporate chain of command. Digital Equipment Corporation, a highly successful manufacturer of minicomputers from the 1960s through the 1980s, looked at the PC—with its substantially different customer, CVP, margin structure, channel to market, and manufacturing requirements—and pronounced it a non-dog. CEO Ken Olsen wasn't interested in selling computers piecemeal; he wanted to own the entire computing structure of his customers' enterprises. DEC actually had a PC under development in its laboratory and eventually sank $2 billion into the effort, but by the time the poor cat received the serious resource commitment it needed, it was too late.

Similarly, in 1975 Kodak engineer Steve Sasson invented the first digital camera, which captured low-resolution black-and-white images and transferred them to a TV. At the time, Kodak was the dominant maker of photographic film. Perhaps fatally, he dubbed it "filmless photography" when he demonstrated the device for various leaders at the company. "After taking a few pictures of the attendees at the meeting and displaying them on the TV set in the room," says Sasson, "the questions started coming. Why would anyone ever want to view his or her pictures on a TV? How would you store these images? What does an electronic photo album look like?"[1] Later, Sasson recalled management's overall assessment of the development: "It was filmless photography, so management's reaction was, 'that's cute—but don't tell anyone about it.'"[2] Kodak non-dogged it. Though Kodak's research labs produced brilliant technologies, the products languished. "It seems Kodak had developed antibodies against anything that might compete with film," says Bill Lloyd, Kodak's former chief technical officer.[3] It took more than twenty-five years for Kodak to find success in the digital-camera market with its Easyshare brand. But the device came too late to save the entire enterprise from disruption.

The second danger is the organizational urge to cram new opportunities into the existing business model. Let's call this tendency *dogging the cat*. "Your new cat venture calls for furry mice to fulfill its play needs," says the well-intentioned product happiness manager, "but we have a state-of-the-art stick supply chain and an advanced throwing system we believe will be more economical."

The stick system *is* more economical. But the cats couldn't care less about it. Unhappy, they don't purr or pounce. Instead, they grow neurotic and start scratching the furniture. No one wants to buy a crazy cat, so the whole cat idea is scrapped. Or, if the idea does make it to the market, the cat-that-fetches is such a strange animal that no one buys it. It matches no one's job-to-be done.

Dogging the cat can also be viewed as the business version of a process that is all too familiar in government. Laws are written to do one thing but come out of the legislative sausage factory looking entirely different. To gain the support of the many people who must vote to ratify the bill, it is amended, weakened, and sometimes changed until everyone's best intentions create a Frankenstein's monster.

Let's say an observant manager sees an unmet need in a market and writes a nifty CVP describing how to meet it. The new CVP enters the system, and the influential design group hears about it. That group lends its support but introduces a small change to keep the proposition within existing design paradigms. Then the marketing organization gets on board—with a few changes to make the CVP more appealing to the existing customer base. The powerful finance group revises the pricing, margins, and cost basis to conform to "what makes us great." And on it goes until the result is a product or service that serves no one's needs at all.

As originally conceived, for example, the US Army's Bradley Fighting Vehicle was to be a light, fast armored personnel carrier capable of moving a dozen or so troops into and out of a theater of operations quickly and safely. That was before a succession of Pentagon generals, inculcated with the military's core-model predisposition for highly complex systems, dogged the Bradley into a combination troop carrier, scout vehicle, and antitank weapon platform. To accommodate its tank-killing weaponry, troop capacity was reduced to six. To reach scouting speed, its hull was made of lightweight, vulnerable aluminum.[4] Seventeen years of development and $13 billion later, those conflicting specifications produced "a troop transport that can't carry troops, a reconnaissance vehicle that's too conspicuous to do reconnaissance, and a quasi-tank that has less armor than a snow blower but carries enough ammo to take out half of D.C."[5] A live-fire test finally exposed its weaknesses; a single shell annihilated it.

Even within a highly innovative culture like Hilti's, the temptation to dog the cat is almost irresistible. "In a fleet process," explains Hilti sales and marketing head Marco Meyrat, "you define the spot in the life cycle of a tool when it should be replaced, and we were refreshing tools before they broke down. Our business unit, whose habitual thinking was to extract maximum value from our investments, suggested that we extend the life of the tool in the fleet. But this very natural thought jeopardized the value proposition of the fleet management program. If our customers were not getting the latest technology and their tools were breaking down more frequently, they would begin to wonder whether they were getting good value from the contract."[6]

Assaults on nascent initiatives can be less subtle. Sometimes, someone just wants to kill the cat. If the core organization is suddenly struggling to meet its numbers or must address a major operational problem or a growth opportunity that needs more resources, any new initiative that isn't yet self-supporting can face sudden death. Entrenched departments often worry about cannibalization; they fear that the new cat could become a dog-eating tiger, consuming critical resources and endangering the entire kennel. Or if the core organization runs out of patience and expects the new venture to grow at the pace and on the scale of the traditional core-growth initiatives, the venture can be shut down or brought back into the mainstream organization to face a slower but just as certain death.

This is precisely what happened to a project, aptly named Kittyhawk, at Hewlett-Packard in the early 1990s. The Kittyhawk team, a part of HP's disk memory division, had embarked on a disruptive play with a 1.3-inch hard disk drive, a cat that was a far cry from even the smallest 3.5-inch dog in HP's pack. The Kittyhawk was meant to be a "small, dumb, cheap" disk drive that could power diminutive devices like the Nintendo Game Boy and personal digital assistants for UPS drivers, a whole new market. But the disk memory division was impatient for growth: it had its sights set on the big dogs at IBM and Seagate and wanted to bulk up quickly. So it projected second-year revenue growth of $100 million, a highly ambitious number. This projection did not give the Kittyhawk team the time it needed to explore the Nintendo opportunities and other promising propositions as they came along. Having been set up to fail, Kittyhawk did, and the project was shut down by 1994, just over two years after its initial launch.[7]

THE PROBLEM OF EXISTING RULES, NORMS, AND METRICS

The DogCorp metaphor is a lighthearted way to illustrate the things people do in the service of their existing business model. These impulses are often implicit, arising not as direct imperatives of the model but in response to the business rules, behavioral norms, and related success metrics that have developed to allow the model to be executed effectively, repeatedly, and efficiently. These invisible guardians of the prevailing business model are essential for managing and executing operations and innovation efforts focused on growing the core or pursuing adjacencies. But they are poison to new business models.

The established norms of a business can limit how far a project team will venture from traditional offerings, precluding new approaches to what can be sold (such as moving from a product to a service) or how an offering can be sold (such as moving from physical stores to the internet). When fundamentally new CVPs

FIGURE 35

Common rules of thumb derived from the core business model that interfere with the requirements of the new business model

Financial	Operational	Marketing/Sales/R&D/HR
Gross margins	End-product quality	Pricing
Opportunity size	Supplier quality	Performance demands
Unit pricing	Owned vs. outsourced manufacturing	Product-development life cycles
Unit margin	Customer service level	Basis for individuals' rewards and incentives
Time to break even	Channel options	Brand parameters
Net present value calculations	Lead times	
Credit terms	Throughput	

are devised, established rules can prevent the changes in the profit formula or in key resources and processes that are needed to make it thrive.

The Locked Nature of the Profit Formula

Those financial pit bulls? They are merely acting to protect the company's current profit formula. Expected margins of the core enterprise, for example, can lead executives to reject out of hand the possibility of reinventing a business model around a different margin model. They may reject an innovation even if the other parts of the profit formula could be changed to describe a potentially profitable white-space play—say, by coupling lower margins with lower overhead, lower cost structures, and higher resource velocity. The rigidity inherent in the existing cost structure, especially when it comes to overhead, together with the challenges involved in making structural changes to the resource velocity of the business, make it difficult for a business unit to accept initiatives that require new unit margin targets.

When Marco Meyrat brought the new fleet management service to his financial analysts at Hilti, he encountered just this sort of subtle resistance. "Our finance people thought there was too much unknown risk of tool loss and repair costs," he says, "so they took a—how shall I say—very safe view toward pricing. I had to work to keep it affordable. If you price a new offering too high, you kill it before it starts."[8] When Hilti expanded the model to markets outside Switzerland, the finance team again tried to increase pricing without regard for the overall value of the CVP. Again, Meyrat struggled not only to maintain the integrity of the business model innovation but also to prove its value to Finance. "There are always yes-but-ers," he says, "who find a reason to say 'but.'"

Don Sheets at Dow Corning encountered similar problems during the incubation of Xiameter. Finance shot down his early profit formula because it called for smaller margins than Dow Corning's core high-touch sales and solution business. Not until he developed a model that maintained something close to those high margins and dramatically lowered costs to achieve the reduced target price point did he win the department's support. It was an end-around run that luckily succeeded, but the showdown could have just as easily stopped the project in its tracks.

The financial officers in these examples did not take unreasonable positions; they were just unable to conceive of new profit formulas. One error frequently encountered when people are considering new growth opportunities is something Clay Christensen has dubbed the *doctrine of marginal costs*.[9] Faced with a new business proposition that requires capital investment in new capabilities or infrastructure, finance people will commonly respond, "Why would we build this new thing when the marginal cost of utilizing our existing capacity is half or a third of that? Why build a new machine when the existing machine still has some more room to do stuff?" They are looking at the minimal variable costs of producing new products using an existing machine, but they fail to consider the large, already-amortized investment in it. So creating a new product from a new machine seems very expensive because they must factor in the investment in capital and the associated new capabilities. The marginal-cost comparison is accurate on its face, but comparing the costs of the new model to the possible profits of extending the old one is comparing apples to grapes. The conclusion that it should necessarily cost less to use an existing sales force to sell a lower-margin product than to train an entirely new one arises from the same sort of mistaken reasoning.

This financial analysis is even more destructive when it fails to consider the possibility that the new idea could disrupt and replace the old profit formula entirely. The Big Steel companies failed to accurately assess how the more profitable business model of the mini-mills, which used electric-arc furnaces, went on to decimate their business. By ignoring the sunk costs of existing infrastructure when calculating the returns from marginal growth—and not accounting for the disruptive costs of doing nothing—the steel companies used incorrect numbers that make it impossible to do something new.

The Illogic of Leveraging Core Capabilities

The existing key resources and processes that underpin the core model can exert a profound influence on managers who keep the enterprise going on a daily basis. They often try to leverage their core capabilities, whether or not these competencies serve the new model. For example, Sony engineers had a cultural aversion to hard-drive technology, which they found inelegant, so they were reluctant to pursue the MP3 space. Kodak initially ran away from filmless imaging. Of course, white-space plays don't exclude exploiting existing capabilities—the iPod is a hardware/software integration product right in Apple's wheelhouse—but new business models must be free to borrow what they need from the core and reinvent the rest.

The rules of an established model are particularly toxic to a new one because they frequently look like sound business reasons to avoid the unknown. It can be hard to recognize how time-honored norms can impede new growth, and even leaders most aware of the rules' influence can unwittingly fall prey to their restrictive effect. A few years back, I worked with a newly acquired company whose parent understood that the new company had a different business model that required a different way of operating. Even so, the parent company required the new managers to adhere to 150 business rules and related metrics—which kept the acquired firm's leaders traveling to more internal meetings than visits with customers.

REDEFINING THE RULES

No one can serve two masters, the saying goes, and when a company ventures into its white space with a new business model that carries a different set of rules and metrics from those of the core, everyone must be clear about which set of rules should be followed. Otherwise, people will face an impossible conflict of interest. Worse, different people will resolve this conflict differently, which will undermine the organization in unpredictable ways.

Middle managers who are working on a new business innovation project and who have not been explicitly released from the rules governing the core business rarely think that it is in their best interests—or the best interests of their organizations—to embrace the new business model. It's not that they are inherently antagonistic to the new thing, but they don't believe they've been discharged from their responsibility to the old thing. Business-unit heads who are charged with carrying out the core business may find it difficult to know how they can do that while making room for a new initiative as well.

What's more, while an innovation project's expectations about profitability and growth may clearly differ from those of the core, people's compensation packages, promotions, bonuses, and recognition are often tied not to any project, new or old, but to the near-term success of the broader company. This arrangement might be perfectly reasonable for the organization's parts that are working to sustain incremental growth, but business model innovations are inherently uncertain. It's hard to predict how long they'll take to generate substantial revenue streams, and they are more prone to failure than are innovation moves within the core. Who can blame a rational up-and-comer for thinking, "If I do something inconsistent with the way I'm measured, I'll miss my marks"?

Unfortunately, companies rarely allow for more than one career path within a function. Nor do they allow two sets of reward systems to coexist within the corporation, let alone within a business unit. Inhibitors to innovation like these are deep-seated and are almost never exposed to the light of day, a tendency identified by leadership expert Steven Kerr in his classic essay "On the Folly of Rewarding A, While Hoping for B."[10]

The types of innovation-killing and change-phobic behaviors described in this chapter are often blamed on lower-level employees. Explicitly delineating the two sets of rules that the two business models require can resolve a lot of unnecessary conflict and risk-avoidance behavior on their part. The rules governing the core business model are necessary and workers honor them, as they should. They should keep on doing so until senior executives explicitly replace the rules with a new business model built on a CVP and profit formula that are so different that the model requires new processes and resources and, in turn, new rules.

ADDRESSING CHALLENGES AT THE TOP

For the sake of simplicity, I've written about business model innovation as it would occur in the simplest of companies—that is, in an organization with only one offering attached to only one business model. But of course, many, many companies operate as corporations with more than one business unit, each with its own uniquely honed business model. In this sense, a corporation does not have a business model; it is a collection of business models. In my observation, it's nearly impossible for a business unit to adopt and operate more than one business model at a time and do them both well. So when a business unit's model has run its course, not only the business model but also the business unit itself dies off. The life of the corporation continues, but it is carried on in the other ongoing business units and through the creation of new units with new models. Only by continuously creating, operating, trading, and closing business units (and their associated business models) can corporations stay vibrant, continue to grow, and remain relevant to customers who have real, important, and changing jobs-to-be-done.[11]

This is the context in which senior leadership must view the challenges of business model innovation. Like their business-unit counterparts, top leaders must learn to recognize and overcome the influence of existing core business models in the pursuit of their corporation's white spaces. Upper management is paid to grow the corporation. It's also charged with managing risk. For many, white-space pursuits appear overly risky because they lie outside the core or close adjacencies of any of their business units. Past failures from directionless stabs into the white space can become permanently lodged in institutional memory. "We've tried this before and it didn't work," says the once-burned executive, unable to see that the previous failure was caused by the absence of a structured approach. The odds of success are greatly increased if executives understand how the imperatives of the new model differ from those of the existing one.

Cannibalization concerns may be heightened for leaders who make the ultimate decisions about new initiatives. To support a project that at first blush seems to put an existing business at risk requires an unusual mindset, one that thoroughly understands how all four boxes in the business model framework function. Creating a new model for a new job does not have to mean that the current model is threatened or should be changed. A new model can reinforce and complement the core business, as Dow Corning discovered.

Leaders, too, are often uncomfortable not knowing how quickly a white-space opportunity will reach its full potential. A predisposition for fast-growing "bamboo" opportunities can make slow-growing oak tree seedlings seem insignificant and unworthy of further support. New models should be profitable early on but will probably not yield high revenue until their scale accelerates. Leadership teams habituated to managing for the short term can easily become impatient for growth, killing a young project with long-term potential in their search for faster returns.

When leaders are uncomfortable pursuing something new, how can they ever expect anyone else in the company to do so? To seize the white space, leaders must learn to balance the company's investment in sustaining growth with direct investment in new value propositions that require new business models. They must authorize the formation of teams capable of creating these models and then protect and nurture them. Such teams should not be large, but they do have to be focused mainly on the new venture. Members shouldn't be asked to split their time between core and new growth efforts. And the teams need the freedom to establish their own business rhythm—and not conform to the prevailing ways that things are done. Innovation teams must have the authority to relax the rules of the core and then develop new rules and metrics that support the new CVP. That authority can only come from the top.

STRATEGY AND BUSINESS MODELS

Harvard Business School historian Alfred Chandler famously argued that "structure follows strategy."[12] Many senior managers believe that the business structure necessary for a new strategy will somehow naturally evolve. They are frequently disappointed. In fact, in both strategic planning and reality, strategy follows from structure. As we now understand, the structure that executes a strategy is governed by the imperatives of its business model.

Most companies develop their corporate strategy in a deliberate, annual operational exercise that focuses on incrementally improving the core. Strategic initiatives arising from core-based assumptions, however, most often return core-based strategies. This is what is fundamentally broken about most strategic-planning efforts. Within an operational exercise, the capabilities of the core business model limit what strategies can be considered.

Organizations that are looking to grow in new ways need to create a strategy development process that is unfettered from the assumptions that drive its core. To open up their organizations to transformational possibilities, leaders must stop peering through the lens of their traditional CVP, their established profit formula, and their current combination of resources and processes and truly embrace Chandler's prescription.[13]

For structure to follow strategy, the strategy development team must begin with the root of how value is created—the customer. It must identify the critical, unsatisfied jobs of current and potential customers before deciding how best to achieve the company's growth objectives. The team should then consider how to pursue those objectives with a set of real options, one or more of which completely reimagines the business model, changing the game within its industry, transforming existing markets, or creating new ones.

The leadership team should then converge on the appropriate strategy, articulating the types of innovation projects that are suitable for project teams to tackle. In this way, white-space initiatives are melded with overall corporate strategy. Strategy development must remain a flexible, creative process; leaders must make a conscious effort to keep the rules and norms of the core in abeyance while they allow their strategy team to imagine new growth and renewal through business model innovations.

Leadership ultimately answers to a broad assortment of stakeholders, including board members, analysts, and investors. Many leaders become gun-shy when faced with investors who are impatient for growth and wary of new business initiatives that stray too far from the core. "Every new business we've ever engaged in has initially been seen as a distraction by people externally, and sometimes even internally," says Amazon CEO Jeff Bezos. "They'll say, 'Why are you expanding outside of media products? Why are you going international? Why are you entering the marketplace business with third-party sellers?' These are fair questions. But they all have at their heart one of the reasons that it's so difficult for incumbent companies to pursue new initiatives. It's because even if they are wild successes, they usually have no meaningful impact on the company's economics for years."[14]

These questions arise because companies large and small have often failed in the past, leaving investors and analysts skittish. Wall Street prefers safe, stick-to-your-knitting strategies. Unfortunately, even when executives spot a fantastic growth opportunity in their white space, they often don't know how to articulate the new value proposition and how the organization will fundamentally change to support it. They are stymied in their attempts to justify a set of financials so foreign to the norm. So, the analysts penalize the company with a negative report.

It needn't be so. Using the business model framework, leaders could make their plans for seizing transformational growth opportunities less of a mystery to stakeholders of all kinds. The goal would not be just to set expectations about the prospects for new initiatives but to set them within the larger corporate context.

With that in mind, you could start, as I did in this book, by explaining to stakeholders the problem of the growth gap—that is, the reason your company needs to move past its core and adjacencies, why remaining too close to home is actually a greater risk than a well-managed trip into your white space. Then you need to explicate a corporate strategy that includes how you plan to continue your existing CVP growth while embarking on new growth, specifying how much you plan to invest in business model innovation. At this point, you are not advocating one course of action or another. You should be open to all sorts of alternatives to your current models. If you are open, so too will your company be open to thinking about a portfolio of truly breakthrough CVPs.

The dogs that guard the gates of innovation are many and varied, and they often lurk there in disguise. But leaders who are ever vigilant for the challenges that incumbency places in their way—who embrace and communicate the necessity of business model innovation—can make it safely past those challenges and move into the profitable white spaces that lie within, between, and beyond them.

Epilogue

*The world is moving so fast nowadays that
the man who says it can't be done is generally
interrupted by someone doing it.*

—attributed to Elbert Hubbard

Peter Drucker once said, "Every organization . . . has a theory
of the business . . . Some theories of the business are so powerful that they last for a long time. But . . . they don't last forever,
and, indeed, today they rarely last for very long at all. Eventually every theory of the business becomes obsolete and then
invalid."[1] Indeed, the average life span of those theories grows
shorter every day. Building a great business and operating it well
no longer guarantees you'll be around in a hundred years, or even
twenty. In 1965, the average length of time a company remained
on the S&P 500 was thirty-three years. By 1990, it had dropped
to twenty years; in 2012, it was just eighteen. Based on the 2017
churn rate, it is forecast that half of the S&P 500 will be replaced
over the next ten years.[2]

In the twenty-first century, investing for the long term means continually building and rebuilding your organization. Shorter business life cycles require a new sort of management discipline that is capable of leading an organization through a continual process of transformation and renewal. To thrive in today's marketplace, to be built to last, every business must be built to transform.

To be built to transform requires the courage to focus on delivering value for the customer first. Identifying value begins by thinking of important unserved or underserved jobs that customers want to have done and then coming up with well-defined value propositions to address them, however foreign to your current offerings the propositions may be. As Jeff Bezos put it, "If you want to continuously revitalize the service that you offer to your customers, you cannot stop at what you are good at. You'd have to ask what your customers need and want, and then, no matter how hard it is, you'd better get good at those things."[3] With a well-defined CVP serving a focused, well-articulated job, business leaders and project teams can work together to design the appropriate profit formulas, key resources, and key processes the company needs to thrive.

To accomplish these tasks, business leaders need to become business model thinkers, to understand that both the current model underpinning their existing business and any new models they may devise are complex systems with interdependent elements that must work together to deliver real value. To build these systems, they must think like architects or engineers, beginning with blueprints, building prototypes, and developing working structures that can deliver on new areas of opportunity. Although they can't devise all the answers up front, they can ask the right questions. Then they must pursue those answers as an artist would, exploring within a process of structured creativity that allows everyone involved to freely imagine the possible, not just the easily done.

Business model innovation efforts should be focused on the pursuit of something grand—changing the game in an existing market, creating a whole new market, transforming an entire industry. If leaders can't succinctly articulate how a new business model will capture an opportunity for significant corporate growth (or in the face of tectonic shifts, how it will become a powerful engine of company renewal), then white-space efforts or fundamental business model change is unjustified. Business model innovators should be hunters of big game and leave the harvesting of core assets to others.

But while thinking big is an essential precondition for seizing the white space, it is equally imperative to start small. Slowly incubating the new venture using foothold markets will protect it as it grows and matures, giving it the time and space that's needed to test assumptions, make adjustments, and develop the key resources and processes that will deliver the greatest value.

Ultimately, companies need to learn how to get out of their own way. To many, this will seem like the hardest challenge, but I believe that much of the frustration leaders, managers, and employees encounter in trying to do something new stems from an insufficient understanding of the old. Too many companies don't actually know which business models they're operating under. They go along day to day using rules of thumb, incentives, and the odd success story to guide them. But organizations that explicitly understand the elements that make up their current business models are far better positioned to judge how well equipped they are to capitalize on new opportunities or to meet coming threats.

Business model innovation thrives in cultures of inquiry, environments in which new value propositions and ideas for new business models are met with interest and encouragement. In built-to-transform companies, managers recognize that a nascent business opportunity, no matter how non-dog it is, might be the key to the next big thing. "Controlling innovation is an oxymoron," says Netflix CEO Reed Hastings. "You inspire innovation. You support innovation. Unlike the quality process, where the goal is to reduce variability, innovations require you to look for ways to increase variability. And business model innovation is scary because it is the toughest to take on."[4]

It doesn't have to be. Throughout this book, I have detailed a structured approach to the essentially unstructured process of creating something new. I have shown that while forays into your white space carry a high degree of uncertainty, they needn't carry a high level of risk. An organization can make business model innovation into a management discipline—a repeatable process that can be well understood.

Seizing your white space begins with a simple four-box business model framework, but it leads to far-reaching implications for every organization that is navigating the turbulent waters of twenty-first-century global commerce. Business model innovation can help companies meet many of the big challenges they face, whether the concerns are growth gaps, market shifts, revolutionary technologies, or uncontrollable social forces. It can help companies devise profitable, market-based solutions to the needs of consumers and societies all over the world—solutions that will improve people's lives and make their economies more prosperous. To create new growth, spur transformations, and renew our companies, we must learn to seize the white space through business model innovation.

NOTES

CHAPTER 1

1. "Lockheed-Martin 'Skunk Works' P791," video, November 21, 2007, www.youtube.com/watch?v=W3n5cUaG5fg.

2. "Hovercraft in Military Operations," *HoverWorld Insider*, March 2006, www.worldhovercraft.org/insider/mar06.htm#military.

3. David E. Rosenbaum, "Arms Makers and Military Face a Wrenching New Era," *New York Times*, August 4, 1991, www.nytimes.com/1991/08/04/us/arms-makers-and-military-face-a-wrenching-new-era.html.

4. Clayton M. Christensen and Michael E. Raynor, *The Innovator's Solution: Creating and Sustaining Successful Growth* (Boston: Harvard Business School Press, 2003), ch. 9.

5. Chris Zook and James Allen, *Profit from the Core: Growth Strategy in an Era of Turbulence* (Boston: Harvard Business School Press, 2001); Chris Zook, *Beyond the Core: Expand Your Market without Abandoning Your Roots* (Boston: Harvard Business School Press, 2004); Chris Zook, *Unstoppable: Finding Hidden Assets to Renew the Core and Fuel Profitable Growth* (Boston: Harvard Business School Press, 2007).

6. Owen W. Linzmayer, *Apple Confidential 2.0: The Definitive History of the World's Most Colorful Company*, 2nd ed. (San Francisco: No Starch Press, 2004), 68; "Dangerous Limbo at Apple," *BusinessWeek*, July 21, 1997.

7. Kiran Venkatesh, Best Data CABO MP3 Player, March 12, 2000, https://www.anandtech.com/show/501/4.

8. In fact, iTunes music may be a loss leader for the company. Of the $0.99 Apple collected per song, about two-thirds went to the music label, and another 22 percent went to credit-card processing, leaving Apple about a dime to cover the cost of the site and other direct and indirect costs (noted in David B. Yoffie and Michael Slind, "Apple Computer, 2006," Case 9-706-496 [Boston: Harvard Business School Publishing, 2007], 14).

9. Data on Apple's iTunes and iPod was gathered by the author in January 2018 from an aggregate of sources, including internal Innosight research, Apple 10k 2003–2010, and ycharts.

10. Randy Stross, "How the iPod Ran Circles around the Walkman," *New York Times*, March 13, 2005.

11. Data on business model innovation was gathered by the author in March 2017 from an aggregate of sources, including internal Innosight research and Datastream.

12. Data on business model innovators was gathered by the author in March 2017 from an aggregate of sources including internal Innosight research, Reuters, and Google Finance.

13. Zhenya Lindgardt and Margaret Ayers, "Driving Growth with Business Model Innovation," *BCG [Boston Consulting Group] Perspectives*, October 8, 2014, bcgperspectives.com/content/articles/growth_innovation_driving_growth_business_model_innovation.

14. Donna J. Bear et al., *The Quest for Innovation: A Global Study of Innovation Management 2006–2016* (New York: American Management Association, 2006), 74.

CHAPTER 2

1. Adapted from Konstantin Stanislavsky and Elizabeth Reynolds Hapgood, *An Actor Prepares* (1936; reprinted New York: Taylor & Francis, 1989), 177–181.

2. Peter Drucker, "The Theory of the Business," *Harvard Business Review*, September–October 1994, 95–104.

3. Joan Magretta, *What Management Is: How It Works, and Why It's Everyone's Business* (New York: Free Press, 2002), 46.

4. See, for example, Henry William Chesbrough, *Open Business Models: How to Thrive in the New Innovation Landscape* (Boston: Harvard Business School Press, 2006); and Henry William Chesbrough, *Open Innovation: The New Imperative for Creating and Profiting from Technology* (Boston: Harvard Business School Press, 2003).

5. Key resources and processes can also be termed *company capabilities* or, organized in a certain way, can be used to describe the value chain of a business.

6. The term *jobs-to-be-done* was coined by Gage Foods CEO Richard Pedi, and the concept has been greatly extended by Clay Christensen and others. See, for instance, Clayton Christensen, David Duncan et al.,

Competing against Luck: The Story of Innovation and Customer Choice
(New York: Harper Business, 2016).

7. Theodore Levitt, "Marketing Myopia," *Harvard Business Review*
(Best of HBR 1960), July 2004, 1–13.

8. Christensen and Raynor, *Innovator's Solution: Creating and Sustaining Successful Growth* (Boston: Harvard Business School Press, 2003),
99n17.

9. Of course, now many people have removed their landlines and rely
solely on their mobile phones.

10. Peter Drucker, *Managing for Results* (New York: Collins, 1993), 94.

11. Charles D. Ellis, Anne M. Mulcahy, and Joel M. Podolny, *Joe Wilson
and the Creation of Xerox* (Hoboken, NJ: John Wiley & Sons, 2006), 196.

12. Sometimes, high prices create value for customers (exclusive residential enclaves, golf course memberships, and art masterpieces come to
mind), but these cases are far from common.

13. "Heart Attack Kills One Person Every 33 Seconds in India," *India
Times*, May 19, 2016; "Heart Disease No. 1 Killer of Indians," *DNAIndia
.com*, July 28, 2013.

14. Nancy F. Koehn and Katherine Miller, "John Mackey and Whole
Foods Market," Case 9-807-111 (Boston: Harvard Business School Publishing, 2007), 9.

15. Clayton Christensen and Richard S. Tedlow, "Patterns of Disruption
in Retailing," *Harvard Business Review*, January–February 2000, 42–45.

16. Ronald Fink, "Forget the Float? The 2001 Working Capital Survey," *CFO Magazine*, July 1, 2001, www.cfo.com/article.cfm/2997693.

17. William A. Sahlman and Laurence E. Katz, "Amazon.com: Going
Public," Case 9-899-003 (Boston: Harvard Business School Publishing,
1998), 22.

18. Phillip Elmer-DeWitt, "How to Grow the iPod as the MP3 Player
Market Shrinks," *CNN Money*, January 29, 2008, http://apple20.blogs
.fortune.cnn.com/2008/01/29/beyond-the-incredible-shrinking-ipod-
market.

19. "iTunes 'Biggest US Music Seller,'" *BBC News*, April 4, 2004, http://
news.bbc.co.uk/2/hi/business/7329886.stm.

20. "Healthy Heart for All: 2013 Edison Awards," YouTube, April 24,
2013, www.youtube.com/watch?v=rUOJtqjLgc4.

21. John R. Wells and Travis Haglock, "Whole Foods Market, Inc.,"
Case 9-705-476 (Boston: Harvard Business School Publishing, 2005), 5–6.

22. Koehn and Miller, "John Mackey and Whole Foods Market," 8.

23. Yuichiro Kanematsu, "Foxconn, Apple and the Partnership That Changed the Tech Sector," *Nikkei Asian Review*, July 13, 2017.

24. Thomas M. Box and Kent Byus, "Ryanair (2005): Successful Low Cost Leadership," *Journal of the the International Academy for Case Studies* 12, no. 2 (2005), 10–11.

25. Wells and Haglock, "Whole Foods Market," 8.

26. "Company History," n.d., www.wholefoodsmarket.com/company/ history.php; Samuel Sen, "Whole Foods Market: To Be or B2B" (Austin, TX: McCombs School of Business, fall 2001), 1.

CHAPTER 3

1. "Highlights from the History of Dow Corning Corporation, the Silicone Pioneer," Dow Corning Corporation, Form No. 01-4027-01, 2007.

2. C. K. Prahalad and M. S. Krishnan, *The New Age of Innovation: Driving Co-Created Value through Global Networks* (New York: McGraw-Hill, 2008), 199.

3. David J. Morrow, "Statement on Breast Implant Claims," *New York Times*, November 10, 1998.

4. The discussion of Dow Corning in this chapter comes from Don Sheets, corporate vice president and chief financial officer of Dow Corning, interview by author, November 1, 2006; and Dan Futter, senior vice president of commercial and consumer experience of Dow Consumer Solutions, interview by author, April 13, 2017.

5. Clayton M. Christensen, *The Innovator's Dilemma: When New Technologies Cause Great Firms to Fail* (Boston: Harvard Business School Press, 1997), 183; Geoffrey A. Moore, *Crossing the Chasm* (New York: HarperBusiness, 1991). Companies can compete and differentiate on more than one level of performance. For the purpose of this conversation, I am focused on the primary basis of competition.

6. Stephen E. Lin and Enrico Senger, "Case Study Xiameter: E-Commerce Solution Covering Business Customer Ordering and Information Processes," case study (Hanover, NH: Center for Digital Strategies at Tuck School of Business at Dartmouth, and St. Gallen, Switzerland: Institute of Information Management, 2003).

7. Ron Fillmore, global executive director of Xiameter, interview by author, tape recording from phone interview, October 18, 2006.

8. The discussion of Hilti in this chapter comes from Marco Meyrat, member of the executive board and head of worldwide sales and marketing at Hilti, interview by author, June 17, 2008.

9. Pius Baschera, interview by author, tape recording from phone interview, June 3, 2008.

10. "Fred Smith on the Birth of FedEx," The Great Innovators/Online Extra, *BusinessWeek*, September 20, 2004, www.businessweek.com/maga zine/content/04_38/b3900032_mz072.htm.

11. Amar V. Bhidé, *The Origin and Evolution of New Business* (Oxford: Oxford University Press, 2000), 185.

CHAPTER 4

1. Rekhu Balu, "Strategic Innovation: Hindustan Lever Ltd.," *Fast Company*, May 2001.

2. Information on Hindustan Unilever gathered by author on June 10, 2009, from http://finapps.forbes.com, under Hindustan Unilever, "Income Statements" and "Ratios and Returns."

3. Nitin Paranjpe, interview by author, tape recording from phone interview, July 11, 2008.

4. V. Kasturi Rangan and Rohithari Rajan, "Unilever in India: Hindustan Lever's Project Shakti—Marketing FMCG to the Rural Consumer," Case 9-505-056 (Boston: Harvard Business School, 2002), 6; 2001 Census of India.

5. Paranjpe, interview.

6. Scott Anthony, Mark W. Johnson, Joseph V. Sinfield, and Elizabeth J. Altman, *The Innovator's Guide to Growth: Putting Disruptive Innovation to Work* (Boston: Harvard Business Press, 2008), 48–59.

7. Ming Zen and Peter J. Williamson, "The Hidden Dragons," in *Harvard Business Review on Doing Business in China*, ed. Kenneth Lieberthal (Boston: Harvard Business School Press, 2004), 68.

8. Justin Lahart, Patrick Barta, and Andrew Batson, "New Limits to Grow Revive Malthusian Fears," *Wall Street Journal*, March 24, 2008.

9. Govind Rajan, interview by author, tape recording from phone interview, June 27, 2008.

10. Ibid.

11. Ibid.

12. Paranjpe, interview.

13. As the initiative later achieved scale and market acceptance, margin levels increased.

14. Paranjpe, interview; Unilever, "Expanding Opportunities in Our Value Chain: Shakti—Driving Opportunity & Sales," Unilever web page, 2018, www.unilever.com/sustainable-living/enhancing-

livelihoods/opportunities-for-women/expanding-opportunities-in-our-
value-chain/index.html.

15. Krishnendu Dasgupta, interview by author, tape recording from
phone interview, July 2, 2008.

16. Sanjiv Kakkar, interview by author, tape recording from phone
interview, June 24, 2008.

17. Chris Trimble, "Hindustan Lever," Case 2-0011 (Hanover, NH: Tuck
School of Business at Dartmouth, 2002).

18. Kakkar, interview.

19. Dasgupta, interview.

20. "Marketing to Rural India: Making the Ends Meet," India Knowledge @ Wharton (2007), 2–3; and Rangan and Rajan, "Unilever in India."

21. Dasgupta, interview.

22. Paranjpe, interview.

23. Ibid.

24. Unilever, "India: Creating Rural Entrepreneurs," Unilever web
page, https://www.unilever.com/Images/es_project_shakti_tcm244-
409741_en.pdf.

25. Dasgupta, interview; and Kakkar, interview.

26. Dasgupta, interview.

27. "From Homemakers to Breadwinners: Shakti Ammas Are Leading the Way," https://brightfuture.unilever.com/stories/482407/From-
Homemakers-to-Breadwinners-Shakti-Ammas-are-Leading-the-Way.aspx.

28. Clayton M. Christensen, Jerome H. Grossman, and Jason Hwang, *The
Innovator's Prescription: A Disruptive Solution for Health Care* (New York:
McGraw-Hill, 2009), 312–313.

29. Sarah A. Leavitt, "A Thin Blue Line: The History of the Pregnancy
Test Kit," National Institutes of Health, December 2003, https://history
.nih.gov/exhibits/thinblueline/index.html.

30. Jon Cohen, *Coming to Term: Uncovering the Truth about Miscar-
riage* (Boston: Houghton Mifflin, 2005), 28–29.

31. Leavitt, "Thin Blue Line."

32. These basic archetypes are outlined in both Charles B. Stabell and
Øystein Fjeldstad, "Configuring Value for Competitive Advantage: On
Chains, Shops, and Networks," *Strategic Management Journal* (May 1998):
413–437; and Geoffrey A. Moore, "Strategy and Your Stronger Hand,"
Harvard Business Review, December 2005, 62–72.

33. This general framework is addressed by Øystein Fjeldstad and
Geoffrey Moore but with some difference in language. Fjeldstad uses the
term *solution shops*, whereas Moore prefers *complex operations*.

34. In describing this framework, Fjeldstad, Moore, and Christensen use slightly different terms. Fjeldstad uses *value chains*, Christensen prefers *value-adding process*, and Moore employs the term *volume operations*.

35. Steve Wunker, "Get the Job Done," *Strategy & Innovation* 3, no. 4 (July–August 2005): 11–13.

36. https://www.cvs.com/minuteclinic/visit/about-us/history.

37. Christensen, Grossman, and Hwang, *Innovator's Prescription*, 166.

38. Joseph L. Bower and Clark Gilbert, "Pandesic: The Challenges of a New Business Venture (A)," Case 9-399-129 (Boston: Harvard Business School, 1999); and Joseph L. Bower and Clark Gilbert, "Pandesic: The Challenges of a New Business Venture (B)," Case 9-399-130 (Boston: Harvard Business School, 1999).

39. Clayton Christensen and Michael Raynor, "How to Pick Managers for Disruptive Growth," *Harvard Business School Working Knowledge*, October 13, 2003.

CHAPTER 5

1. Peter J. Williamson and Ming Zeng, "Value-for-Money Strategies for Recessionary Times," *Harvard Business Review*, March 2009, 66–74.

2. Clayton M. Christensen, *The Innovator's Dilemma: When New Technologies Cause Great Firms to Fail* (Boston: Harvard Business School Press, 1997), 24.

3. Ibid., 87–93.

4. Internal research conducted by the author and Innosight in an analysis of approximately 350 business model innovations.

5. Farhad Manjoo, "While We Weren't Looking, Snapchat Revolutionized Social Media," *New York Times*, November 30, 2016.

6. Shai Agassi, interview by Kristian Steenstrup, February 2009, https://www.gartner.com/doc/942913.

7. Max Chafkin, "A Broken Place: The Spectacular Failure of the Startup That Was Going to Change the World," April 7, 2014, *Fast Company*, www.fastcompany.com/3028159/a-broken-place-better-place.

8. Ibid.

CHAPTER 6

1. Amazon, *2002 Annual Report*; and *2008 Annual Report*, http://phx.corporate-ir.net/phoenix.zhtml?c=97664&p=irol-reportsannual.

2. Scott D. Anthony and Evan I. Schwartz, *The Transformation 10: Strategic Change Rankings for 2017*, Innosight, 2017, www.innosight.com/wp-content/uploads/2017/05/Innosight_Transformation-10.pdf.

3. Bloomberg, "How Amazon Opens Up and Cleans Up," Special Report: Will Web Services Click?, *BusinessWeek*, June 24, 2003.

4. Taylor Soper, "Amazon Web Services Posts $3.5B in Sales, Up 47% from Last Year, Reaches $14B Annual Run Rate," *GeekWire*, February 2, 2017, www.geekwire.com/2017/amazon-web-services-posts-3-5b-revenue-47-last-year.

5. Although Amazon does not disclose sales figures, Citigroup analyst Mark Mahaney has projected that 2008 Kindle sales were approximately 500,000, as noted in Douglas MacMillan, "Amazon Kindle 2: No iPod for Books," *BusinessWeek*, February 10, 2009.

6. Jeff Bercovici, "Amazon vs. Book Publishers, by the Numbers," *Forbes.com*, February 10, 2014, www.forbes.com/sites/jeffbercovici/2014/02/10/amazon-vs-book-publishers-by-the-numbers/#5f651a2f4ef9.

7. Dan Frommer, "Why Microsoft Stock Is at an All-Time, 31-Year High," *Recode*, July 21, 2017, www.recode.net/2017/7/21/16008618/microsoft-all-time-stock-price-chart.

8. Richard Waters, "Microsoft Recruits Help in Strategy Shift," *Financial Times*, June 13, 2016, www.ft.com/content/6c48312e-3182-11e6-ad39-3fee5ffe5b5b.

9. Microsoft, *2017 Annual Report*, https://www.sec.gov/Archives/edgar/data/789019/000156459017014900/msft-10k_20170630.htm.

10. GE, *2015 Annual Report*, www.ge.com/ar2015/assets/pdf/GE_AR15.pdf.

11. GE, "HBR on GE's Revolutionary Evolution," *GE Digital* (blog), n.d., was written about the following article: Marco Iansiti and Karim R. Lakhami, "Digital Ubiquity: How Connections, Sensors, and Data Are Revolutionizing Business," *Harvard Business Review*, November 2014, https://hbr.org/2014/11/digital-ubiquity-how-connections-sensors-and-data-are-revolutionizing-business.

12. Steve Blank, "Why GE's Jeff Immelt Lost His Job: Disruption and Activist Investors," *Harvard Business Review*, October 2017, https://hbr.org/2017/10/why-ges-jeff-immelt-lost-his-job-disruption-and-activist-investors.

13. James B. Stewart, "Netflix Looks Back on Its Near-Death Spiral," *New York Times*, April 26, 2013, www.nytimes.com/2013/04/27/business/netflix-looks-back-on-its-near-death-spiral.html.

14. Ibid.

15. Janko Roettgers, "Netflix's Latest Streaming Record: Members Viewed 250 Million Hours of Video on a Single Day in January," *Variety*, March 16, 2017, http://variety.com/2017/digital/news/netflix-250-million-hours-1202010393.

16. Leo Sun, "Is Netflix Inc. a Growth Stock or a Cult Stock?," *Fox Business*, January 25, 2017, www.foxbusiness.com/markets/2017/01/25/is-netflix-inc-growth-stock-or-cult-stock.html.

CHAPTER 7

1. The following case study comes from an actual project undertaken by Innosight, although company names have been changed for purposes of confidentiality.

2. Or, if you must start with an existing product, the question is not "What do you need from my product?" but rather "What is my product for, and is it the best way to do that job?"

3. Clayton M. Christensen and Michael E. Raynor, *The Innovator's Solution: Creating and Sustaining Successful Growth* (Boston: Harvard Business School Press, 2003), 75–79.

4. Scott Anthony, Mark W. Johnson, Joseph V. Sinfield, and Elizabeth J. Altman, *The Innovator's Guide to Growth: Putting Disruptive Innovation to Work* (Boston: Harvard Business Press, 2008), ch. 4.

5. "Zara, a Spanish Success Story," *CNN.com*, June 15, 2001, http://edition.cnn.com/BUSINESS/programs/yourbusiness/stories2001/zara.

6. Miguel Helft, "Fashion Fast Forward," *Business 2.0*, May 2002.

7. Nirmalya Kumar, "Zara: Spanish Season," *Businessworld*, October 2005, www.businessworld.in/index.php/Spanish-season.html.

8. Max Chafkin, "The Customer Is the Company," *Inc.*, June 2008.

9. Ibid.

10. Joseph V. Sinfield, Edward Calder, Steve Colson, and Bernard McConnell, "How to Identify New Business Models," *Sloan Management Review* (Winter 2012), https://sloanreview.mit.edu/article/how-to-identify-new-business-models/

11. I am indebted to Rita McGrath and Ian MacMillan for their elegant formulation of the reverse income statement. See Rita Gunther McGrath and Ian C. MacMillan, *The Entrepreneurial Mindset: Strategies for Continuously Creating Opportunity in an Age of Uncertainty* (Boston: Harvard Business School Press, 2000).

12. Pankaj Ghemawat and José Luis Nueno, "Zara: Fast Fashion," Case 9-703-497 (Boston: Harvard Business School Publishing, 2003), 9.

13. Scott Anthony, Clark Gilbert, and Mark Johnson, *Dual Transformation: How to Reposition Today's Business While Creating the Future* (Boston: Harvard Business Review Press, 2017).

CHAPTER 8

1. The idea of the three stages of implementation comes from a lecture by David Garvin on behalf of Intel's new-business initiatives group on February 18, 2008, at the Harvard Business School.

2. Rita Gunther McGrath and Ian C. MacMillan, "Discovery-Driven Planning," *Harvard Business Review*, July–August 1995, 44–54.

3. Scott Cook, quoted in "A Formula for Failure," *BusinessWeek* Playbook, July 10, 2006.

4. Scott Cook, comments given at Meeting the Growth Imperative forum, Boston, August 7, 2008.

5. Ibid.

6. Scott Anthony, Mark W. Johnson, Joseph V. Sinfield, and Elizabeth J. Altman, *The Innovator's Guide to Growth: Putting Disruptive Innovation to Work* (Boston: Harvard Business Press, 2008), 149.

7. Reed Hastings, comments given at Meeting the Growth Imperative forum, Boston, August 7, 2008.

8. Rigas Donganis, *The Airline Business in the Twenty-First Century* (London: Routledge, 2001), 132.

9. Vijay Govindarajan and Julie B. Lang, "Southwest Airlines Corporation," Case 2-0012 (Hanover, NH: Tuck School of Business at Dartmouth, 2002), 1–2.

10. Julia Kirby and Thomas A. Stewart, "The Institutional Yes: An Interview with Jeff Bezos," *Harvard Business Review*, October 2007, 74–82.

11. Pankaj Ghemawat and José Luis Nueno, "Zara: Fast Fashion," Case 9-703-497 (Boston: Harvard Business School Publishing, 2003), 15.

12. Ibid.

13. Inditex spokesperson for Zara, interview by the author, tape recording from phone interview, May 27, 2008.

14. Krishnendu Dasgupta, interview by author, tape recording from phone interview, July 2, 2008; and Sanjiv Kakkar, interview by author, tape recording from phone interview, June 24, 2008.

15. Vijay Mahajan, "How Unilever Reaches Rural Consumers in Emerging Markets," *Harvard Business Review*, December 14, 2016.

16. Terry Kelly, comments given at Meeting the Growth Imperative forum, Boston, August 7, 2008.

17. Don Sheets, interview by author, November 1, 2006.

18. Brad Anderson, comments given at Meeting the Growth Imperative forum, Boston, August 3, 2007.

19. See, for example, Ronald N. Ashkenas and Suzanne C. Francis, "Integration Managers: Special Leaders for Special Times," *Harvard Business Review*, November–December 2000, 108–116; and Larry Selden and Geoffrey Colvin, "M&A Needn't Be a Loser's Game," *Harvard Business Review*, June 2003, 70–79.

20. John Deighton, "How Snapple Got Its Juice Back," *Harvard Business Review*, January 2002, 47–53.

21. Jim Mateja, "How Chrylser Marriage Failed," *Chicago Tribune*, May 15, 2007.

22. Vijay Govindarajan and Chris Trimble, *Ten Rules for Strategic Innovators: From Idea to Execution* (Boston: Harvard Business School Press, 2005), 6.

23. Anderson, comments, Meeting the Growth Imperative forum.

24. Best Buy website, https://www.bestbuy.com/site/electronics/geek-squad/pcmcat138100050018.c?id=pcmcat138100050018.

CHAPTER 9

1. Steve Sasson, "PluggedIn: A Blog about Kodak Products and Customers," October 16, 2007, http://stevesasson.pluggedin.kodak.com/default.asp?item=687843.

2. Claudia H. Deutsch, "At Kodak, Some Old Things Are New Again," *New York Times*, May 2, 2008.

3. Ibid.

4. W. Blair Haworth, *The Bradley and How It Got That Way: Technology, Institutions, and the Problem of Mechanized Infantry in the United States Army* (Westport, CT: Greenwood Press, 1999), 28, 78.

5. From the film *The Pentagon Wars*, as cited in Michael A. Prospero, "Build an Army for Your Ideas," *Fast Company*, June 2006.

6. Marco Meyrat, interview by author, tape recording from phone interview, June 17, 2008.

7. Clayton M. Christensen, "Hewlett-Packard: The Flight of the Kittyhawk (A)," Case 9-606-088 (Boston: Harvard Business School Publishing, 2006).

8. Meyrat, interview.

9. Clayton M. Christensen, Stephen P. Kaufman, and Willy C. Shih, "Innovation Killers: How Financial Tools Destroy Your Capacity to Do New Things," *Harvard Business Review*, January 2008, 98–105.

10. Steven Kerr, "On the Folly of Rewarding A, While Hoping for B," *Academy of Management Journal* 18, no. 4 (December 1975): 769–783.

11. Richard Foster and Sarah Kaplan, *Creative Destruction: Why Companies That Are Built to Last Underperform the Market—and How to Successfully Transform Them* (New York: Currency, 2001), 162.

12. Alfred D. Chandler, *Strategy and Structure: Chapters in the History of the American Industrial Enterprise* (Cambridge, MA: MIT Press, 1990), 14.

13. Joseph L. Bower and Clark G. Gilbert, "How Managers' Everyday Decisions Create—or Destroy—Your Company's Strategy," *Harvard Business Review*, February 2007, 72–79.

14. Julia Kirby and Thomas A. Stewart, "The Institutional Yes: An Interview with Jeff Bezos," *Harvard Business Review*, October 2007, 74–82.

EPILOGUE

1. Peter F. Drucker, "The Theory of the Business," *Harvard Business Review*, September–October 1994, 95–104.

2. Scott D. Anthony et al., "Corporate Longevity Forecast: The Pace of Creative Destruction Is Accelerating," *Innosight Executive Briefing*, January 2017.

3. Jeff Bezos, interview by author, tape recording from phone interview, October 27, 2008.

4. Reed Hastings, comments given at Meeting the Growth Imperative forum, Boston, August 7, 2008.

INDEX

ACKNOWLEDGMENTS

I have been pondering the question of business models and business model innovation almost since I began Innosight with my friend and colleague Clayton Christensen over fifteen years ago. In a meeting Clay had with former Intel CEO Andy Grove in 1999, Grove rightly pointed out that disruptive threats came inherently not from new technology but from new business models. Since then, we have realized that disruptive innovation and business model innovation were opposite sides of the same coin. But that led to some questions: What really is a business model? And how do you create a truly new one? The words *business model innovation* have been bandied about, particularly since the internet boom of the late 1990s, but no one had come up with any satisfying framework from which to work.

Then in 2005, my client and good friend Dan Pantaleo, a vice president in global communications at SAP AG, asked me to help him identify the most pressing issues that the company's senior clients and executives should be focusing on for the future. We immediately converged on business model innovation as the issue that most needed to be better defined and understood. We collaborated for almost two years, deeply researching several companies we deemed business model innovators and holding a series of CEO summits on the topic. The work led ultimately to "Reinventing Your Business Model," the McKinsey Award–winning *Harvard Business Review* article that I wrote with Clay Christensen and former SAP CEO Henning Kagermann. Throughout, Dan was an invaluable colleague, always willing to engage deeply in the hard task of understanding the real challenges involved in transformative growth and renewal through business model innovation.

From these early efforts arose many more questions, which led me to write this book. In it, I have attempted to describe business models in a simple framework that can be easily grasped and applied to new business model development. I've then attempted to apply the framework to the cases I've studied firsthand. This research forms the core of the book.

Right now, companies around the world, in both developed and developing countries, are reinventing their business models. Through the stories of the companies I've researched in depth, I have sought to bring the power and the possibilities of the business model framework to life. I don't wish to suggest that this framework is the only way to think about business models. Rather, I offer it as a useful lens through which to view your white space as a less scary place and to make the reinvention of business models a predictable, well-managed process. For this reason, I hope the framework will be applicable not just to private-sector businesses but also to many other institutions—NGOs, government agencies, defense contractors—that need to respond to changing circumstances or may be frustrated in their attempts to capitalize on new opportunities.

The long journey from conceptualization to writing a book could not have been completed without the help of a host of people.

In addition to Dan Pantaleo of SAP, I am grateful to my coauthor on the HBR article, Henning Kagermann, and to the dedicated support of Herbert Heitmann and Stacy Comes at SAP Global Communications.

Special thanks go to Karl Ronn, John Leikham, and George Glackin at Procter & Gamble. They have given me extensive feedback and guidance on the business model framework over the years. They've also been kind enough to engage in hours of spirited dialogue and debate about how to make business models and business model innovation relevant to practitioners.

Scott Cook, chairman of Intuit, provided invaluable input in reviewing versions of both the HBR article and various parts of the manuscript. His comments are always so rich in insight and pushed my thinking tremendously.

Nelson Handel, a delightfully creative and gifted storyteller, helped me enormously in the sometimes mystical task of taking the story out of my head and putting it on paper. Nelson spent countless hours talking with me about the ideas, assisting with the research, doing yeoman's work on the initial drafts, and working with me through innumerable iterations, remaining ever patient and vigilant to make sure we told the story right.

I also extend my deep appreciation to the numerous colleagues who graciously gave their time to review all or part of the manuscript and whose comments I found invaluable: Vivek Bapat of SAP; Peter Blackman and Dominique Fournier of Infineum; Stefan Bockamp of E.ON AG; Bob Boyd, Isen Disken, and Neil Kacena of Lockheed Martin; Larry Burns and Tony Posawatz of GM; Kim Clark of Brigham Young University–Idaho; Roy Davis, Michelle Goodridge, Jack Groppel, Calvin Schmidt, and Harlan Weisman of Johnson & Johnson; Chris Fleck of Citrix Systems; John Gatti of BAE Systems; Hang Chang Chieh of National University of Singapore; Tarun Khanna and Willy Shih of Harvard Business School; Susan Marcinelli of Best Buy; Steve Milunovich of Merrill Lynch; Steve Spear of MIT; Gary Williams of wRatings Corporation; and Tom Wilkerson of the US Naval Institute. Clement Chen of SAIC and Russ Conser of Shell gave particularly detailed and insightful comments, which significantly advanced my thinking in many parts of the book.

My colleagues at Innosight, each and every one of them, past and present, have taught and continue to teach me every day.

Particular thanks go to Josh Suskewicz, who was instrumental early on in the business model research, as well as to former colleagues Alex Leichtman and Lilac Berniker. Alex Slawsby and Jennifer Gaze also provided very helpful research and support. Thoughtful reviews of the manuscript came from Ryan Fisher, Tim Huse, Dave Goulait, and Andy Waldeck. Steve Wunker provided indispensable contributions in the development of early chapter drafts. Ned Calder and Joe Sinfield were very helpful with their contributions in the development of chapter 7, "Designing a New Business Model." Andrea Ovans provided outstanding editorial contributions. She was ever insistent that I state things precisely and with brevity, and I am extremely grateful for her efforts to preserve a clear line of logic through and through. I also greatly appreciate Eileen Roche, Janice Evans, and Renee Callahan's careful, exacting review of the manuscript, and Daniel Guidera's high-quality contributions to the development of all the graphics. Judi Haviland and HBR's Karen Player also provided a very helpful eye in shaping the graphics.

I'm deeply indebted to my primary editors at Harvard Business Press: former editor Hollis Heimbouch, who got me on my way, having enough faith to sign me on as an author, and Jacque Murphy, a marvelous coach who provided lots of encouragement throughout the process. I'm also grateful to Allison Peter and Ania Wieckowski of the Press for their invariably kind assistance.

I owe a very special thanks to Allen Stoddard. Allen shepherded so many important elements of manuscript development and peer review, I really can't commend him enough for his diligence, attention to detail, positive attitude, and willingness to endure long hours to see the book through to completion.

I am especially beholden to my colleagues and fellow Innosight board members Scott Anthony, Matt Eyring, Dick Foster, and

Clark Gilbert for their support while I was writing the book and their extremely perceptive reviews of the manuscript. Through all these years, they have been not only tremendous colleagues but also great friends.

Several colleagues at Innosight were of immense help in this update. Tim Riser and Stefan Pate conducted insightful research and helpful advice in providing the relevant updates. Cathy Olofson and Evan I. Schwartz provided very useful reviews and suggestions on the updated manuscript. Arthur Goldwag was tremendously valuable as a thought partner and gifted writer in putting thoughts to paper. I am grateful to Harvard Business Review Press editor Tim Sullivan for giving me a chance to write this update and to have yet another opportunity to share these ideas with the world.

Clay Christensen's resolute support, his steadfast willingness to listen, and ever-astute review of the work mean more than I can ever adequately capture in words. He is a man of supreme intellect, compassion, and humility. He has taught me what it means to give deeply of oneself, and I am forever grateful for all he has done for me personally and professionally.

I owe a tremendous debt to my lifelong mentor and friend Leo S. Tonkin, Esq., who instilled in me the famous words "The unexamined life is not worth living." His guidance along my life's journey has in so many ways large and small influenced my thinking about the world and about matters both professional and personal. His influence permeates this book, and for that I am forever grateful.

My deepest gratitude goes to my family. My children are a constant source of joy and inspire me to be a better person. My wife, Jane, is my greatest champion and best friend. She has been a tremendous source of wisdom and support throughout the research and writing of this book. As a journalist, she has taught me the power of a story well told, helping me sharpen the manuscript and bring it to life. Above all, Jane has taught me the importance of connecting with and caring for others. Her kindness and finely tuned intuition for people, and truth, have made my life richer and sweeter than I could have ever imagined.

MARK W. JOHNSON is a senior partner of Innosight, a strategy consulting firm focused on advising corporations on creating new growth and managing transformation, which he cofounded in 2000 with Harvard Business School professor Clayton M. Christensen and which was acquired by Huron in 2017. He has consulted to Global 1000 and startup companies in a wide range of industries—including health care, aerospace/defense, enterprise IT, energy, automotive, and consumer packaged goods—and has advised Singapore's government on innovation and entrepreneurship.

The first edition of this book was published by Harvard Business Press in 2010, with the title *Seizing the White Space*. Mark is also a coauthor of the book *Dual Transformation: How to Reposition Today's Business While Creating the Future* (Harvard Business Review Press, 2017), a blueprint for how successful companies can take advantage of disruptive change to fortify their existing business while simultaneously developing new growth engines and *The Innovator's Guide to Growth* (Harvard Business Press, 2008). He is a coauthor of the McKinsey Award–winning *Harvard Business Review* article "Reinventing Your Business Model," as well as numerous articles in *Sloan Management Review*, the *Washington Post*, *Advertising Age*, and *National Defense*.

Prior to cofounding Innosight, Mark was a consultant at Booz Allen Hamilton, where he advised clients on managing innovation and implementing comprehensive change programs. Before that, he served as a nuclear-power-trained surface-warfare officer in the US Navy in the first Gulf War.

Mark received an MBA from Harvard Business School, a master's degree in civil engineering and engineering mechanics from Columbia University, and a bachelor's degree with distinction in aerospace engineering from the US Naval Academy. He currently serves on the board of the US Naval Institute.

Mark, his wife, Jane Clayson Johnson, and their children live in Belmont, Massachusetts.